MW00915043

Incredible Football Stories for Young Readers

15 Inspirational Tales From Football History for Kids

Trevor Fields

© **Copyright Trevor Fields 2024 - All rights reserved.**

The content contained within this book may not be reproduced, duplicated or transmitted without direct written permission from the author or the publisher.

Under no circumstances will any blame or legal responsibility be held against the publisher, or author, for any damages, reparation, or monetary loss due to the information contained within this book. Either directly or indirectly. You are responsible for your own choices, actions, and results.

Legal Notice:

This book is copyright protected. This book is only for personal use. You cannot amend, distribute, sell, use, quote or paraphrase any part, or the content within this book, without the consent of the author or publisher.

Disclaimer Notice:

Please note the information contained within this document is for educational and entertainment purposes only. All effort has been executed to present accurate, up to date, and reliable, complete information. No warranties of any kind are declared or implied. Readers acknowledge that the author is not engaging in the rendering of legal, financial, medical or professional advice. The content within this book has been derived from various sources. Please consult a licensed professional before attempting any techniques outlined in this book.

By reading this document, the reader agrees that under no circumstances is the author responsible for any losses, direct or indirect, which are incurred as a result of the use of the information contained within this document, including, but not limited to, — errors, omissions, or inaccuracies.

Table of Contents

CHAPTER 1:
The First Game: How American Football Began

Imagine a chilly afternoon in November 1869. The leaves were turning brilliant shades of red and gold, and a crisp breeze was whispering that winter was on its way. On this particular day, something extraordinary was about to happen in New Brunswick, New Jersey, something that would change the course of sports history in the United States forever.

On one side of the field stood a team from Rutgers College, dressed in scarlet scarves tied around their heads and waists—these were their "uniforms." Across from them, the team from Princeton University, ready and eager to face off in what many consider to be the very first game of American football.

Now, you might be picturing the football games you see on TV, with helmets, touchdowns, and quarterbacks, but the game played that day was quite different. It looked more like a blend of soccer and rugby than the American football we know today. The ball was round, not the familiar oval shape, and the rules? Well, they were making them up as they went along!

The goal of this first game was simple: to kick the round ball into the opponent's territory and score points, much like in soccer. However, carrying the ball or throwing it wasn't part of the plan—yet. Each team had 25 players on the field at the same time, which might sound like utter chaos, and in some ways, it was!

As the game began, excitement filled the air. The players, most of whom had never played a game like this before, were learning the rules as they played. The spectators, a mix of students and curious onlookers, cheered from the sidelines, wrapped in blankets and sipping on hot beverages to keep warm.

The game was rough and tumble, with players chasing the round ball across the field, kicking it and trying to outmaneuver the opposing team. There were no helmets or pads like the players wear today, just the determination and grit of young men who were part of something new and thrilling.

By the time the game ended, Rutgers emerged victorious with a score of 6 to 4. But more important than the score was the sense of accomplishment and camaraderie among the players. They didn't know it then, but they were the pioneers of American football, laying the foundation for a sport that would grow in ways they could hardly imagine.

This first game sparked an interest that quickly spread to other colleges and universities. Each game played experimented with different rules and ideas, slowly shaping the sport into something closer to the football we know today. But how did we go from a chaotic game with 25 players on each side and a round ball to the structured, strategic sport with oval footballs and specific positions?

As American football began to capture the hearts of players

and spectators alike, a flurry of games followed that first historic match. Colleges across the East Coast started forming their own teams, eager to try out this new sport. Yet, with each game, it became evident that a jumble of improvised rules wasn't enough. Imagine playing a game where each time you show up, the rules change! It was confusing and, frankly, a bit wild.

Enter Walter Camp, a name you might not know but one that's incredibly important in the world of American football. Often called the "Father of American Football," Walter was a former Yale football player who saw the potential in this rough-and-tumble game. But more than that, he saw a future where football could be more than just a chaotic scramble for the ball; it could be a game of strategy, skill, and discipline.

In the late 1870s and early 1880s, Walter Camp began to propose changes to the existing set of rules, changes that would start to shape football into the sport we recognize today. One of his first and most significant contributions? Reducing the number of players on the field from 25 to 11. This wasn't just a random decision; it was a move that aimed to reduce confusion and increase the game's strategic aspects.

Camp didn't stop there. He introduced the concept of a line of scrimmage, which created a clear start point for each play. This was a game-changer—literally. It meant that instead of a wild scramble for the ball, there was now a moment of strategy and anticipation before each play. Teams had to think ahead, plan their moves, and outsmart their opponents.

Another groundbreaking rule introduced by Camp was the system of downs. Initially, teams had three tries to advance the ball five yards. If they succeeded, they got another set of tries. This rule added a layer of tension and excitement to the game, as teams pushed to gain ground within their limited attempts.

With these changes, football started to look more familiar. But there was still something missing—something that would take the game to new heights of excitement and strategy. That something was the forward pass. Initially, football mainly involved running with the ball or kicking it. But as safety concerns grew due to the physical intensity of the game, the idea of throwing the ball forward as a legal play began to gain traction.

The forward pass was officially introduced in 1906, revolutionizing the game. It opened up a whole new dimension of play, allowing for long throws down the field, dramatic catches, and a faster-paced game. It also made football safer, as it reduced the number of pile-ups and intense physical clashes.

As these rules refined the game, football began to grow in popularity, drawing larger crowds and generating more excitement. High schools, colleges, and eventually professional leagues embraced the sport, each adding their layer of tradition and innovation to the game.

The evolution of American football from that first game in 1869 to the structured, strategic sport we know today was a journey of innovation, experimentation, and, above all, a love for the game. Walter Camp's contributions laid the groundwork for modern football, but it was the passion and dedication of countless players, coaches, and fans that propelled the sport forward.

With the essential rules set by Walter Camp and the game becoming more structured, football's popularity started to skyrocket. By the early 20th century, football had become a staple of American culture, especially in colleges across the nation. However, as much as the game was loved, it wasn't without its challenges. Football, in its early days, was a rough sport, leading to injuries and, in some cases, even fatalities. This caused a national debate about the safety of the game and whether it should continue to be played in schools and colleges.

In response to growing concerns over player safety, President Theodore Roosevelt, a fan of the sport and a believer in its value for American youth, stepped in. In 1905, he called representatives from Harvard, Princeton, and Yale to the White House and urged them to make changes to ensure the game's safety. This meeting was a pivotal moment in football history, emphasizing that the sport needed to evolve not just in its play but in its commitment to player well-being.

Following President Roosevelt's intervention, the National Collegiate Athletic Association (NCAA) was established in 1906, primarily to regulate football and enforce new safety measures. This included not only the legalization of the forward pass, which helped to spread out the play and reduce dangerous physical confrontations, but also the introduction of new equipment like helmets and padding.

As football became safer and more regulated, its popularity only continued to grow. The first bowl game, the Rose Bowl, was played in 1916 between Michigan and Stanford, starting a tradition of postseason college football that fans adore to this day. The concept of professional football also began to take shape, with the formation of the American Professional Football Association in 1920, which would later become the National Football League (NFL).

The NFL's formation marked a significant milestone in football's history, transitioning the sport from a college-focused pastime to a professional endeavor with its stars and legends. Names like Red Grange, the "Galloping Ghost," brought attention and fans to the game, showcasing the incredible skill and athleticism of football players to a wider audience.

But professional football wasn't an instant success. In its early years, the NFL struggled to gain the popularity of college football. Games were often played in small towns, and players weren't the celebrities they are today. It took decades, innovations in how the game was played and presented, and the rise of television to bring professional football into the homes and hearts of millions of Americans.

Television, in particular, played a crucial role in football's rise to prominence. The first televised NFL game was in 1939, but it wasn't until the 1950s and 60s, with the advent of color TV and national broadcasts, that football truly became a part of American life. Iconic games, legendary players, and moments of sheer sporting brilliance were now accessible to everyone, creating a shared experience that spanned the entire country.

Football's journey from a rudimentary game played on a college field in New Jersey to a national obsession is a story of innovation, adaptation, and passion. The sport has evolved significantly over the years, but at its heart, it remains a testament to the power of teamwork, strategy, and the relentless pursuit of excellence.

As football's journey continued through the 20th century and into the 21st, the sport saw numerous changes and milestones that have cemented its place in American culture. The Super Bowl, for instance, has become more than just a championship game; it's an annual event that draws millions of viewers from around the world, featuring halftime shows with top musical artists and commercials that are as anticipated as the game itself.

The introduction of new technologies and the internet has transformed how fans interact with the game. Instant replays, high-definition broadcasts, and multiple camera angles have brought viewers closer to the action than ever before. Fantasy football and online streaming services have changed how fans follow their favorite teams and players, making football a year-round conversation.

Statistics have also played a significant role in the evolution of football. With the advent of advanced metrics and analytics, teams can analyze performance and strategy with incredible precision. This data-driven approach has influenced everything from player recruitment to game-day decisions, showcasing the sport's blend of physical prowess and strategic intellect.

Football's impact extends beyond the field, influencing American society in profound ways. It's a sport that brings people together, regardless of background, to share in the excitement and drama of each game. Through youth leagues, high school teams, and college scholarships, football offers opportunities for personal development and educational advancement.

The stories of resilience, teamwork, and triumph that define football are inspirational. Players like Jim Brown, who broke barriers and stood up for civil rights, and Tom Brady, whose dedication to the sport is legendary, serve as role models for young fans. The sport teaches values such as perseverance, discipline, and the importance of working together towards a common goal.

As we close this chapter on how American football began, it's clear that the game is much more than just a sport. It's a part of American identity, a reflection of the country's love for competition, celebration of talent, and, most importantly, a source of shared joy and community. From that first game in 1869 to the modern spectacle of the Super Bowl, football has grown into a beloved tradition that continues to inspire and unite millions.

Football's story is still being written, with new legends to emerge, records to be broken, and moments that will live forever in the hearts of fans. It's a sport that has evolved dramatically from its humble beginnings, but at its core, it remains a testament to human spirit and the joy of competition.

CHAPTER 2:
Jim Brown: A Trailblazer On and Off the Field

In the world of sports, there are legends, and then there's Jim Brown. A name that resonates far beyond the confines of the football field, Brown's story is one of unmatched excellence, unwavering conviction, and pioneering activism. Brown's journey from a young athlete to a national icon offers lessons that go well beyond touchdowns and rushing yards.

Born on February 17, 1936, in St. Simons Island, Georgia, Brown moved to Long Island, New York, at a young age. Here, in the town of Manhasset, his athletic prowess began to shine. Brown wasn't just a football player; he excelled in basketball, lacrosse, and track as well. However, it was on the football field where his combination of speed, strength, and intelligence truly set him apart.

Jim Brown attended Syracuse University, where his athletic talent blossomed. In football, he dominated the game like few before him. In his senior year alone, Brown scored an astonishing 43 points against Colgate, showcasing his remarkable abilities to run, catch, and even kick the football. But

Jim Brown's college career wasn't just about the highlight reels; it was also a time when he began to face and overcome significant challenges.

During the 1950s, America was still grappling with segregation and racial discrimination, and Brown was not immune to these societal challenges. Despite facing prejudice and exclusion, Brown's response was not of bitterness but of excellence. He let his performance on the field speak for itself, breaking records and setting new standards for future generations.

Brown's prowess on the football field was undeniable. By the time he graduated from Syracuse, he had earned a spot in the All-American team, marking him as one of the best college football players in the country. However, Jim Brown's impact was only just beginning. In 1957, he was drafted by the Cleveland Browns, where he would embark on a professional career that would redefine the sport of football.

In his rookie season, Brown led the NFL in rushing yards, a feat he would accomplish eight times in his nine-season career. But perhaps more impressive than his ability to evade defenders and break tackles was Brown's consistency and durability. He never missed a game in his professional career, a testament to his physical conditioning and mental toughness.

Jim Brown's football statistics are staggering. He rushed for 12,312 yards, scored 106 touchdowns, and averaged an incredible 5.2 yards per carry over his career. But Jim Brown was more than his stats. He was a player who could single-handedly change the outcome of a game, a player whose mere presence on the field commanded respect and attention.

Yet, Jim Brown's influence extended far beyond the gridiron. Even at the peak of his athletic career, Brown was keenly aware of the social injustices that plagued America. He understood the platform he had as a prominent athlete and chose to use it to advocate for change, equality, and empowerment for African Americans.

As Jim Brown's career with the Cleveland Browns soared, so did his awareness of the power he wielded beyond the end zones. Brown wasn't just playing a game; he was setting stages, breaking barriers, and challenging norms in a society that was deeply divided by racial lines. His excellence in football granted him a platform, one he didn't take lightly. Brown understood that his success could open doors—not just for himself, but for others in the African American community striving for equality and justice.

In the mid-1960s, at the height of his football career, Jim Brown made a decision that shocked fans and the sports world alike. He announced his retirement from the NFL at just 29 years old, at a time when he was still considered one of the most dominant players in the game. But Jim Brown saw a calling higher than football. He turned his full attention to activism and efforts to uplift African American communities, leveraging his fame to spotlight social issues.

Brown's commitment to change was multifaceted. He founded the Negro Industrial Economic Union, later renamed the Black Economic Union, which aimed to support African American entrepreneurship and provide economic opportunities for black communities. Through this organization, Brown sought to address economic disparities and empower African Americans to achieve financial independence and success.

But perhaps what stands out most in Jim Brown's activism is his leadership in the fight for civil rights. He was not just a participant in the movement; he was a leader, using his voice and stature to bring attention to the struggles and injustices faced by African Americans. Brown organized and participated in summits that brought together athletes and entertainers to discuss and plan actions for social change. One of the most famous of these was the 1967 Cleveland Summit, which supported Muhammad Ali's stance against the Vietnam War draft, showcasing solidarity among prominent African American athletes in the face of controversy.

Jim Brown's activism wasn't always met with widespread approval. At a time when many expected athletes to "stick to sports," Brown's outspoken nature and commitment to social issues challenged the status quo. Yet, he remained undeterred, understanding that the fight for equality was far more significant than any game.

Brown's influence extended into the realm of film and television, where he pursued a successful acting career. Through roles in films and TV shows, Brown broke down racial stereotypes, portraying characters that defied the limited and often demeaning roles typically offered to black actors at the time. His success in entertainment, much like his success in football, challenged perceptions and opened doors for future generations of African American actors.

Jim Brown's journey from the football field to the forefront of social activism illustrates the profound impact one individual can have in multiple arenas. His legacy is not just that of the greatest football player to ever play the game but also as a pioneering force for social change and racial equality.

Jim Brown's transition from the gridiron to the front lines of activism set a powerful precedent for athletes using their platforms for social change. His efforts off the field were rooted in a deep belief in justice, equality, and the power of community. Brown didn't just lend his voice to the civil rights movement; he rolled up his sleeves and worked to make tangible improvements in the lives of African Americans.

One of the most notable aspects of Brown's activism was his focus on empowering young African Americans through education and sport. He understood the challenges faced by youth in underserved communities, including poverty, lack of access to quality education, and the dangers of gang violence. In response, Brown founded the Amer-I-Can program in 1988, an initiative designed to address these issues by providing life skills, education, and guidance to young people. The program's mission was to help individuals achieve their full potential, regardless of their circumstances.

Amer-I-Can was built on the principle that self-determination, responsibility, and hard work are key to overcoming adversity. Through this program, Brown reached out to thousands of young people, offering them a pathway to success and a chance to redirect their lives towards positive outcomes. His work with Amer-I-Can is a testament to his commitment to making a lasting difference, one life at a time.

Jim Brown's efforts also extended to bridging gaps between rival gangs in Los Angeles during the 1980s and 1990s. At a time when gang violence was at its peak, Brown hosted meetings at his own home, bringing together members from different gangs to negotiate peace and promote unity within the community. His interventions helped reduce violence and fostered a sense of brotherhood among former rivals, showcasing his ability to lead and inspire even in the most challenging situations.

Beyond his direct involvement in activism and community work, Jim Brown's legacy influenced generations of athletes to use their platforms for social causes. He demonstrated that being a professional athlete comes with a responsibility to contribute to the greater good and that fame and influence can be powerful tools for advocating change. Brown showed that it's possible to excel in sports while also standing up for what's right, paving the way for future sports figures to engage in activism.

As we look at the landscape of sports today, the echoes of Jim Brown's impact are evident. Athletes across various sports have taken up the mantle of activism, speaking out on issues ranging from racial injustice to gender equality, inspired by pioneers like Brown who showed them the way. Jim Brown's life serves as a reminder that one's contributions to society can far exceed personal achievements, and that true greatness is measured by the positive impact one has on the world.

Jim Brown's legacy is a rich tapestry that weaves together unparalleled athletic achievement with profound social impact. It's clear that Brown's influence extends well beyond the records he set or the games he won. His true legacy lies in his courage to stand up for what he believed in, his commitment to change, and the countless lives he touched through his activism and philanthropy.

Brown's life teaches us about the power of using one's platform for a greater purpose. He showed us that fame and talent can be leveraged to advocate for equality, uplift communities, and inspire others to act. Brown's work off the field, especially with the Amer-I-Can program, highlights his belief in the potential within each individual to overcome obstacles and achieve greatness, no matter their background or circumstances.

His efforts to mediate gang violence and promote peace in communities torn apart by conflict demonstrate his deep commitment to social justice and his ability to lead and inspire change in the most challenging situations. Brown understood that real strength lies not in physical prowess but in character, integrity, and the willingness to stand up for others.

Jim Brown retired from professional football over half a century ago, but his impact on the sport and society remains indelible. Today, athletes across various disciplines continue to follow in his footsteps, using their voices and resources to fight for justice and equity. From advocating for criminal justice reform to supporting educational initiatives, the spirit of activism that Brown embodied is alive and well in the world of sports.

He serves as a powerful reminder that true greatness is achieved not just by excelling in one's chosen field but by making a positive difference in the world. Brown's journey from the football field to the forefront of social activism showcases the impact one individual can have when they are driven by a commitment to excellence, justice, and compassion.

Jim Brown's story is not just a chapter in the history of football; it's a chapter in the ongoing story of the struggle for equality and justice. It teaches us about the power of conviction, the importance of giving back, and the enduring impact of leaving the world better than we found it. Jim Brown's life offers valuable lessons in courage, leadership, and the relentless pursuit of what is right, lessons that are as relevant today as they were during his time.

CHAPTER 3:
Patrick Mahomes: A New Era of Quarterback

Every so often, an athlete comes along who changes the game. Patrick Mahomes II, with his rocket arm, fearless play, and creative genius, is one of those players. Mahomes has not only captured the hearts of fans but has also ushered in a new era for quarterbacks in the NFL.

Born on September 17, 1995, in Tyler, Texas, Patrick Lavon Mahomes II was destined for sports. His father, Pat Mahomes, was a professional baseball pitcher, which meant Patrick was introduced to the world of professional sports at a very young age. However, it wasn't baseball that captured Patrick's heart; it was football.

From his early days playing youth football to becoming a standout player at Whitehouse High School in Texas, Mahomes demonstrated a natural talent and a deep love for the game. But it wasn't just his arm strength or his ability to make plays that set him apart; it was his extraordinary ability to see and think about the game differently. Even in high school, Mahomes displayed a playing style that was both daring and inventive, traits that would become his hallmark in the years to come.

After high school, Mahomes chose to attend Texas Tech University, where he played college football and baseball. At Texas Tech, Mahomes's football career took off. He became known for his powerful throws, quick decision-making, and ability to execute plays under pressure. In his 2016 season, Mahomes led all NCAA Division I FBS players in multiple categories, including passing yards (5,052) and total touchdowns (53). This remarkable season not only showcased his skills but also set the stage for his entry into the NFL.

In the 2017 NFL Draft, the Kansas City Chiefs made a bold move by trading up to select Mahomes as the 10th overall pick. It was a decision that would reshape the future of the franchise and the league itself. Mahomes spent his rookie year learning from veteran quarterback Alex Smith, a period that proved invaluable for his development.

The 2018 season was Mahomes's breakout year. As the starting quarterback for the Chiefs, he lit up the league with his dynamic plays and fearless leadership, throwing for over 5,000 yards and 50 touchdowns. This phenomenal performance earned him the NFL MVP award, making Mahomes the youngest player to receive the honor since Dan Marino in 1984.

What sets Mahomes apart is not just his impressive statistics but how he plays the game. His no-look passes, sidearm throws, and ability to escape pressure and make plays on the move have redefined what it means to be a quarterback. Mahomes's playing style is a blend of creativity, athleticism, and sheer will to win, traits that have inspired a new generation of players and fans alike.

Patrick Mahomes's impact on the Kansas City Chiefs was immediate and transformative. In his first season as a starter, he led the team to the AFC Championship Game, something the Chiefs hadn't reached in decades. His unique blend of talent, including his uncanny ability to throw the ball with both power and precision, turned the Chiefs into one of the most formidable teams in the NFL.

One of the most memorable moments of Mahomes's early career came during a game against the Baltimore Ravens in 2018. Facing a critical 4th down with the game on the line, Mahomes scrambled to his right, evaded defenders, and, while nearly out of bounds, launched a stunning 48-yard pass across his body to wide receiver Tyreek Hill. This play not only kept the Chiefs in the game but also showcased Mahomes's incredible arm strength and his willingness to take risks, traits that would define his career.

Mahomes's leadership extends beyond his physical abilities. His teammates speak highly of his work ethic, positive attitude, and ability to inspire those around him. It's not just about the touchdowns or the spectacular throws; it's about how Mahomes elevates the entire team, making everyone better. This intangible quality of leadership has been a key factor in the Chiefs' success.

Off the field, Mahomes has also made a significant impact. In 2020, he used his platform to advocate for social justice and voter participation, showing that his influence reaches beyond football. Mahomes understands the responsibility that comes with his status and is committed to making a positive difference in the community.

In addition to his advocacy work, Mahomes has engaged in numerous charitable efforts. He established the "15 and the

Mahomies" Foundation, which is dedicated to improving the lives of children. The foundation's work includes initiatives focused on health, wellness, communities in need, and other charitable causes. Through his foundation, Mahomes has demonstrated a commitment to giving back, reinforcing the idea that he is a leader both on and off the field.

The 2019 season further cemented Mahomes's legacy as one of the greats. He led the Chiefs to Super Bowl LIV, where they faced off against the San Francisco 49ers. In what would become a defining game of his career, Mahomes rallied the Chiefs from a 10-point deficit in the fourth quarter to win the Super Bowl, earning the Super Bowl MVP award in the process. This victory was more than just a championship; it was a testament to Mahomes's resilience, talent, and leadership.

Mahomes's journey from a talented young player to one of the NFL's biggest stars has been remarkable. But what truly sets him apart is his approach to the game. Mahomes plays with a joy and creativity that is infectious, reminding fans and players alike that football, at its core, is about passion, innovation, and the pursuit of excellence.

Patrick Mahomes's influence on football and the quarterback position is profound, setting new standards for what it means to play the game. His ability to perform under pressure, combined with his innovative playing style, has not only led to personal success but has also elevated the Kansas City Chiefs to new heights.

The 2023 Super Bowl against the Philadelphia Eagles was another highlight in Mahomes's already illustrious career. Leading the Chiefs to yet another championship game, Mahomes displayed his signature mix of talent and tenacity. In a game filled with tension and spectacular moments, Mahomes's leadership and skill were on full display, demonstrating why he is considered one of the best quarterbacks in the league. The Chiefs triumphed in a 38-35 win over the Eagles. Mahomes's performance solidified his reputation as a player who rises to the occasion in the biggest moments.

But it was the 2024 Super Bowl that would truly cement Patrick Mahomes as one of the greatest quarterbacks of all time. In a dramatic and unforgettable game against the San Francisco 49ers, Mahomes led the Chiefs to victory in overtime, where Mahomes completed the game-winning touchdown pass to Mecole Hardman to secure the 25-22 Super Bowl win. Mahomes showcased his incredible ability to orchestrate comebacks and make pivotal plays in what was a very close and competitive game. This victory was more than just a triumph; it was a testament to Mahomes's staying power as one of the best to ever do it as his position. The 2024 win gave him his third Super Bowl ring at just 28 years old.

Mahomes's impact on the game extends beyond his achievements in Super Bowls. He has inspired a new generation of quarterbacks and young athletes who see in him a role model and a benchmark for success. Mahomes has redefined what it means to play the quarterback position, blending traditional skills with a modern flair that has made the game more exciting and unpredictable.

His influence is also seen in the way teams across the NFL are now scouting and developing quarterbacks. The qualities that Mahomes embodies—mobility, arm strength, creativity, and the ability to make plays out of nothing—are now highly sought after in up-and-coming players. In this way, Mahomes is shaping the future of the quarterback position, encouraging a more dynamic and versatile approach to playing the game.

Off the field, Mahomes continues to use his platform for positive change. His commitment to community service, social justice, and philanthropy has made him a beloved figure not just in Kansas City but across the country. Through his actions, Mahomes demonstrates that being a great athlete also means being a great person, someone who uses their success to help others and make the world a better place.

CHAPTER 4:
America's Team: The Dallas Cowboys of the 1990s

Few football teams have captured the imagination and hearts of fans around the country like the Dallas Cowboys, especially during the 1990s. This era was a golden age for the team, marked by extraordinary talent, memorable games, and, most importantly, Super Bowl victories that solidified their place in NFL history.

The story of the 1990s Dallas Cowboys is a tale of transformation and triumph. In the late 1980s, the Cowboys were struggling. They were far from the powerhouse they had once been in the 1970s, a time when they first earned the nickname "America's Team." However, the winds of change began to blow in the early '90s, thanks to a few key decisions and some incredibly talented players.

One of the pivotal moments for the Cowboys was the hiring of Jimmy Johnson as head coach in 1989. Johnson, who had found success in college football, brought a new energy and vision to the team. Alongside owner Jerry Jones, Johnson began rebuilding the Cowboys, focusing on acquiring young, dynamic players through the draft and trades.

One of the most significant trades in NFL history occurred in 1989, when the Cowboys traded their star running back, Herschel Walker, to the Minnesota Vikings. In return, the Cowboys received a multitude of draft picks, which they used to build the foundation of their 1990s dynasty. This trade is often seen as a turning point, allowing the Cowboys to draft key players who would become central to their success.

Among these players were Emmitt Smith, Michael Irvin, and Troy Aikman. Aikman, a quarterback from UCLA, was the first overall pick in the 1989 NFL Draft. Michael Irvin, a wide receiver from the University of Miami, was already on the team, having been drafted in 1988. And Emmitt Smith, a running back from the University of Florida, joined the Cowboys as the 17th overall pick in the 1990 NFL Draft. Together, these three would form the core of the Cowboys' offense and become known as "The Triplets."

The early '90s saw the Cowboys rapidly improving. Aikman's leadership, Irvin's ability to make big plays, and Smith's relentless running created a dynamic and potent offense. Meanwhile, the defense, led by players like Charles Haley and Deion Sanders, was becoming just as formidable.

By 1992, the Cowboys were ready to reclaim their spot at the top of the NFL. They finished the regular season with a 13-3 record, dominating their opponents with a balanced attack on both offense and defense. This success carried into the playoffs, where the Cowboys' talent and hard work culminated in a trip to Super Bowl XXVII against the Buffalo Bills.

In that Super Bowl, the Cowboys showcased their

superiority. The game was a decisive victory for Dallas, with Aikman throwing for four touchdowns and the defense forcing a record nine turnovers. The win not only earned the Cowboys their third Super Bowl title but also marked the beginning of a dynasty that would dominate the decade.

The 1990s Dallas Cowboys' story is not just about the victories and the championships; it's about how a team can rise from a period of struggle to achieve greatness. It's a testament to the power of vision, determination, and teamwork. As we continue this chapter, we'll delve deeper into the careers of "The Triplets," the Cowboys' strategy for success, and the legacy of this iconic team.

As the 1990s unfolded, the Dallas Cowboys were not just a football team; they were a phenomenon. The blend of skill, strategy, and star power made them a force to be reckoned with on the field and beloved figures off it. At the heart of this powerhouse were the players who became legends in their own right, each bringing something unique to the team.

Emmitt Smith, the Cowboys' running back, was known for his incredible agility and toughness. Smith wasn't the biggest player on the field, but what he lacked in size, he made up for with heart and determination. He had a remarkable ability to find gaps in the defense, often turning what looked like a small opening into a significant gain. Over the decade, Smith became the NFL's all-time leading rusher, a record that speaks volumes about his consistency and durability. His performances were pivotal in the Cowboys' playoff runs, including their Super Bowl victories.

Michael Irvin, also known as "The Playmaker," was the Cowboys' wide receiver who could always be counted on to make big plays in crucial moments. Irvin combined speed with exceptional catching ability, making him a constant threat to defenses. His connection with quarterback Troy Aikman was legendary; the duo seemed to have an unspoken understanding on the field, leading to some of the most memorable touchdowns in Cowboys history.

Troy Aikman, the quarterback, was the leader on the field. Aikman's strength lay in his precision and intelligence. He wasn't just throwing the ball; he was making strategic decisions, reading the defense, and choosing the best plays to lead his team to victory. Aikman's leadership was a calming presence for the team, especially in high-pressure situations like the Super Bowl.

Beyond "The Triplets," the Cowboys' success in the 1990s was also due to their formidable defense. Charles Haley was a force to be reckoned with, known for his ability to sack the quarterback and disrupt the opposing team's plays. Then there was Deion Sanders, also known as "Prime Time," one of the most versatile athletes in the NFL. Sanders excelled as a cornerback and was a threat on special teams, known for his incredible speed and ability to make game-changing plays.

The Cowboys' coaching staff also played a crucial role in their success. Jimmy Johnson, who led the team to two Super Bowl victories, was known for his motivational skills and sharp football mind. After Johnson, Barry Switzer took over as head coach and led the Cowboys to their third Super Bowl win of the decade in Super Bowl XXX. The transition between coaches could have been a challenge, but the strength and unity of the team ensured continued success.

The 1990s Dallas Cowboys were more than just a collection of talented individuals; they were a team in the truest sense of the word. Their ability to work together, trust in each other's abilities, and execute their game plan was what made them stand out. They played with a confidence and flair that captivated fans, earning them the title of "America's Team."

The Dallas Cowboys' journey through the 1990s was marked by unforgettable games that have since become part of NFL lore. These moments not only defined the Cowboys' dominance but also captured the drama and excitement that make football America's favorite sport.

One such game that stands out is the 1992 NFC Championship Game against the San Francisco 49ers, a matchup between two of the decade's most formidable teams. This game was a test of wills, pitting the Cowboys' rising stars against the seasoned veterans of the 49ers. The victory by the Cowboys, led by Aikman's precision passing, Smith's relentless running, and Irvin's key receptions, was a statement to the league: the Cowboys were back, and they were here to stay. The win propelled them into Super Bowl XXVII, where they clinched their first championship of the '90s.

Super Bowl XXVII against the Buffalo Bills is another game that remains etched in the memory of Cowboys fans. The Cowboys' overwhelming victory, marked by their explosive offense and a defense that forced a record nine turnovers, showcased the team's exceptional talent and teamwork. Aikman's superb performance earned him the Super Bowl MVP, further solidifying his status as one of the game's great quarterbacks.

However, the Cowboys' journey wasn't without its challenges. The 1994 NFC Championship Game against the 49ers presented a hurdle the Cowboys couldn't overcome. In a reversal of fortunes from their previous encounter, the 49ers emerged victorious, ending the Cowboys' quest for a third consecutive Super Bowl title. This loss was a reminder of the narrow margins between victory and defeat in the NFL and served as motivation for the team to come back stronger.

The resilience of the Cowboys was on full display in the 1995 season, which culminated in their victory in Super Bowl XXX against the Pittsburgh Steelers. This win was a testament to the team's ability to rebound from disappointment and achieve greatness. The Cowboys' third Super Bowl victory of the decade was a crowning achievement for the team and reinforced their status as the era's defining dynasty.

The players who made up the 1990s Dallas Cowboys left an indelible mark on the franchise and the NFL. Players like Darren Woodson, Jay Novacek, and Daryl Johnston, though not as widely celebrated as "The Triplets," were instrumental in the team's success. Their contributions, often behind the scenes, helped to create a balanced and unstoppable force on both sides of the ball.

The legacy of the 1990s Dallas Cowboys extends beyond their Super Bowl victories. It's found in the way they captured the imagination of fans across America, with a style of play that was both effective and exhilarating. They were a team that youngsters idolized and aspiring football players wanted to emulate.

The Cowboys' story is a vibrant chapter in the history of American football, a decade that redefined the team's legacy and left an indelible mark on the NFL. Their success on the field brought joy to countless fans and inspired a new generation of players who saw in the Cowboys a model of excellence and determination.

The legacy of the Cowboys from this golden era extends beyond their victories and the championships they secured. It's about the spirit they embodied, a spirit of resilience, innovation, and an unwavering commitment to teamwork. They showed that success is not just about the talent of individual players but about how those players come together to achieve a common goal.

The Cowboys of the 1990s also reminded us of the importance of leadership, both on the field and on the sidelines. Players like Troy Aikman, Emmitt Smith, and Michael Irvin led by example, pushing themselves and their teammates to perform at their best. Similarly, coaches like Jimmy Johnson and Barry Switzer played pivotal roles in shaping the team's mentality and guiding them to success, proving that visionary leadership is just as crucial as physical skill in the pursuit of greatness.

One of the most significant aspects of the Cowboys' legacy is their contribution to the broader culture of football. They helped popularize the game, not just in America but around the world, showcasing the drama, excitement, and athletic excellence that football can offer. The Cowboys of the 1990s were more than just a team; they were a cultural phenomenon, a source of inspiration, and a symbol of the enduring appeal of American football.

It's clear that their impact goes beyond the records they set or the trophies they won. They taught us valuable lessons about perseverance, the importance of embracing challenges, and the power of a united team. Their story encourages us to strive for excellence in all we do and to remember that with hard work, dedication, and a strong team spirit, incredible achievements are within reach.

Today, the legacy of the 1990s Cowboys continues to influence the NFL. Current players and teams look to the Cowboys as an example of what can be accomplished through talent, hard work, and teamwork. The story of America's Team in the 1990s is a testament to the timeless values that underpin the great game of football, values that continue to inspire and motivate everyone who loves this sport.

As we close this chapter on the Cowboys of the 90s, we celebrate not only their triumphs but also the joy and excitement they brought to the game of football. Their legacy remains a beacon for future generations, a reminder of what can be achieved when talent meets determination and teamwork, making their story an enduring part of the rich tapestry of NFL history.

CHAPTER 5:
The Iron Bowl: Auburn vs. Alabama's Fierce Rivalry

In the heart of the southern United States, where college football is not just a sport but a way of life, there lies a rivalry so intense, it divides families, friends, and the entire state of Alabama. This is the story of the Iron Bowl, the annual clash between the Auburn University Tigers and the University of Alabama Crimson Tide, two powerhouses of college football.

The Iron Bowl is more than just a game; it's a tradition that dates back over a century, with the first matchup taking place in 1893. The rivalry is named after Birmingham, Alabama, once the center of the nation's iron and steel industry, where many of the early games were played. Over the years, this fierce competition has become one of the most anticipated events in college football, drawing attention from fans all across the country.

From the outset, the Iron Bowl was marked by its intensity and the high stakes both on and off the field. The rivalry is deeply ingrained in the culture of Alabama, where you're often asked to pick a side—Auburn or Alabama—at a young age. This game is the culmination of a year's worth of bragging rights, community pride, and sometimes, the deciding factor in conference championships or even national title hopes.

One of the most memorable Iron Bowl moments came in 1982, a game affectionately known as "Bo Over the Top." In this game, Auburn's freshman running back, Bo Jackson, leaped over the top of the pile into the end zone for the game-winning touchdown, snapping Alabama's nine-game winning streak in the series. This play is often replayed in the minds of Auburn fans and serves as a symbol of the determination and spirit that defines the rivalry.

Over the decades, the Iron Bowl has been the stage for many unforgettable moments in college football history. From last-second field goals to game-changing plays, the intensity of the rivalry brings out the best in players, coaches, and fans alike. The outcomes of these games are often unpredictable, adding to the excitement and drama that surrounds the annual matchup.

In the Iron Bowl, legends are born, heroes are made, and history is written with each passing year. The rivalry between Auburn and Alabama is a testament to the passion, the rivalry, and the love for college football that runs deep in the heart of the South.

The Iron Bowl has seen countless memorable games and players who have left an indelible mark on the rivalry's history. Each contest is a chapter in the storied tradition, with moments of triumph and heartbreak that have defined generations of fans.

One such game that stands tall in the annals of Iron Bowl history is the 2010 matchup, famously known as "The Camback." Auburn, led by quarterback Cam Newton, who would go on to win the Heisman Trophy that year, found themselves trailing

Alabama 24-0 in Tuscaloosa. What followed was one of the greatest comebacks in college football history. Newton and the Tigers mounted a relentless charge, ultimately winning the game 28-27. This victory kept Auburn's national championship hopes alive, and they would go on to win the BCS National Championship that season. Newton's performance in this game—his leadership, poise, and incredible athleticism—cemented his legacy as one of Auburn's all-time greats.

Another unforgettable moment came in 2013, in a game that would simply be remembered as "The Kick Six." With the game tied at 28 and just one second left on the clock, Alabama attempted a long field goal to win the game. The kick fell short, and Auburn's Chris Davis caught the ball deep in his own end zone. What happened next was nothing short of miraculous. Davis ran the length of the field, 109 yards, for a touchdown as time expired, giving Auburn a stunning 34-28 victory. This play not only sealed the win for Auburn but also became one of the most iconic moments in sports history, symbolizing the unpredictability and sheer excitement of the Iron Bowl.

Through the years, the Iron Bowl has showcased the talents of many exceptional players who have gone on to achieve greatness in college football and beyond. From Alabama's Derrick Henry, who ran for 271 yards in the 2015 game en route to winning the Heisman Trophy, to Auburn's Bo Jackson, a player whose name is synonymous with athletic excellence, the Iron Bowl has been a proving ground for college football's elite.

The rivalry has also been a testament to strategic brilliance and coaching legacies. Legendary Alabama coach Bear Bryant and Auburn's Pat Dye are just two examples of coaches who have left a lasting impact on their programs and the Iron Bowl itself.

Their leadership, along with that of many other great coaches, has shaped the character and direction of their teams, contributing to the lore of the rivalry.

Each game contributes a unique story to the overarching saga of this rivalry. The players and coaches change, but the intensity and passion remain constant, burning as brightly today as it did in the very first matchups.

The 1972 Iron Bowl, often referred to as "Punt Bama Punt," is another legendary chapter in this rivalry's history. With Alabama leading 16-0 and the game nearing its end, Auburn's chances seemed slim. But in a twist of fate that has since become Iron Bowl lore, Auburn's Bill Newton blocked two punts in the final minutes, both of which were returned for touchdowns by David Langner. Auburn's miraculous 17-16 victory over their undefeated rivals is a testament to the unpredictable nature of the Iron Bowl and remains one of the most celebrated moments in Auburn's football history.

Fast forward to 1985, and you find another game that ended in dramatic fashion, known for Van Tiffin's "The Kick." With the game tied and just seconds left on the clock, Alabama's Van Tiffin lined up for a 52-yard field goal attempt. The kick sailed through the uprights, giving Alabama a thrilling 25-23 victory. Tiffin's clutch performance is a highlight reel staple, showcasing the pressure-packed moments that define the Iron Bowl.

In the Iron Bowl, heroes and legends are born in the heat of competition. Take, for instance, Alabama's running back Mark Ingram, who would go on to win the Heisman Trophy in 2009. In the Iron Bowl of that year, Ingram's performance against Auburn was crucial, showcasing his strength and determination as he helped lead Alabama to a come-from-behind 26-21 victory.

This game was a stepping stone for Alabama on their way to a National Championship that season, illustrating how the Iron Bowl can be both a proving ground and a launchpad for greater achievements.

The 2014 Iron Bowl, often called "The Highest Scoring Iron Bowl," was a showcase of offensive firepower. Alabama and Auburn combined for over 1,100 yards of total offense in a game that felt more like a shootout than a traditional football game. Alabama ultimately triumphed 55-44, but the game is remembered for its back-and-forth scoring, incredible plays, and the sheer will of both teams to claim victory. This game emphasized that in the Iron Bowl, expect the unexpected, and no lead is ever safe.

These memorable games and moments are the threads that weave together the rich narrative of the Iron Bowl. With each year, new stories emerge, adding to the legacy of this storied rivalry. Players become legends, and games become folklore, passed down through generations of fans who relish in the history and look forward to the next chapter. As of the end of the 2023 college football season, Alabama led Auburn in the overall Iron Bowl series since 1893 with a record of 50-37 and 1 tie.

The legacy of the Iron Bowl extends far beyond the gridiron. It's a yearly reminder of the power of sports to unite and inspire, to turn neighbors into rivals and then back into friends, celebrating shared passions and respect for the game. It's a day when the state of Alabama stands still, and for a few hours, all that matters is the fierce competition and the pride of two storied programs.

The Iron Bowl is more than just a rivalry; it's a testament to the enduring spirit of the athletes who play and the fans who watch. Each game is a moment in time, a snapshot of determination, skill, and the relentless pursuit of excellence. The stories that emerge from the Iron Bowl – of last-second victories, of unlikely heroes, and of legendary performances – enrich the history of college football and inspire new generations to dream big and work hard.

We celebrate not just the victories and the defeats but the spirit of competition that defines this iconic rivalry. The Iron Bowl reminds us that at the heart of every great sports story are the values of teamwork, resilience, and the unyielding pursuit of excellence. These games teach us about the importance of tradition, the power of community, and the unbreakable bond that sports can create among those who experience it.

The Iron Bowl continues to captivate the imagination of sports fans around the world, serving as a beacon of the passion and excitement that college football offers. Its legacy is not measured by the scores of the games, but by the memories created, the friendships forged, and the spirit of rivalry that brings out the best in everyone involved.

CHAPTER 6:

The Perfect Season: 1972 Miami Dolphins Unbeaten Journey

In 1972, the Miami Dolphins embarked on a journey unlike any other in the history of the National Football League, achieving the only perfect season in its history. Under the brilliant leadership of Head Coach Don Shula, a team comprised of talented individuals united with one unwavering goal: to win every single game, from the sweltering heat of September through the chill of January's Super Bowl.

The Dolphins' remarkable journey was powered by an unparalleled synergy between offense and defense. Quarterback Bob Griese, with his exceptional leadership and tactical intelligence, initially steered the team with precision. However, after Griese suffered a leg injury in Week 5, veteran quarterback Earl Morrall took the helm. Morrall, displaying incredible poise and effectiveness, led the team through the remainder of the regular season, maintaining their unbeaten record.

Miami's offense was a force to be reckoned with, thanks in large part to their formidable running attack, famously known as "Butch and Sundance." Larry Csonka, the bruising fullback, and

Mercury Morris, the swift halfback, became the first duo in NFL history to each rush for over 1,000 yards in the same season. Csonka, with his powerhouse runs, accumulated 1,117 yards and six touchdowns, while Morris added 1,000 yards and 12 touchdowns, showcasing the team's devastating ground game.

The Dolphins' receiving corps, led by wide receiver Paul Warfield, added another dimension to their attack. Warfield, known for his precise route-running and ability to make big plays, tallied 606 receiving yards and scored three touchdowns, providing a constant threat to opposing defenses.

Yet, the Dolphins' journey to perfection wasn't just about their offensive prowess. The "No-Name Defense," so called because of their lack of national recognition, was instrumental in securing the perfect season. This unit, characterized by its disciplined play and cohesive teamwork, was a nightmare for opposing offenses. Nick Buoniconti, the middle linebacker, anchored the defense, while safeties Jake Scott and Dick Anderson patrolled the secondary, each recording significant interceptions that season. The defense allowed only 171 points across the regular season, the fewest in the league, showcasing their dominance on the field.

Throughout the regular season, the Dolphins outmatched every opponent, finishing with a record-setting 14-0 regular-season record. They notched impressive victories, including a pivotal game against the New York Giants in Week 8, where Miami showcased their defensive might by holding the Giants to just 3 points. Another memorable moment came in Week 14 against the Baltimore Colts, where the Dolphins secured their perfect regular season with a convincing 16-0 victory, a game that underscored their readiness for the postseason challenges that lay ahead.

As the regular season concluded, the Dolphins had not only accumulated an unbeaten record but had also set a new standard for excellence in the NFL. The team's combination of a potent running game, a strategic passing attack, and a stifling defense had proven unbeatable. However, the Dolphins knew that their ultimate goal lay ahead: to carry their perfect record through the playoffs and win the Super Bowl, cementing their legacy as one of the greatest teams in NFL history.

As the playoffs dawned in January 1973, the Miami Dolphins, carrying their unblemished record, understood that the hardest part of their journey was still ahead. The postseason would pit them against the strongest teams in the league, each aiming to be the ones to tarnish the Dolphins' perfect record. The first challenge came in the form of the Cleveland Browns in the AFC Divisional Playoff.

The game against the Browns tested the Dolphins' resolve. Miami found themselves in a tight contest, with Cleveland showcasing why they were not to be underestimated. However, the Dolphins' disciplined defense and potent offense proved too much for the Browns. Miami emerged victorious with a 20-14 win, a game that highlighted the team's ability to perform under playoff pressure. Larry Csonka's powerful running was crucial, as he bulldozed through the Browns' defense for critical yards, solidifying his role as a key player in the Dolphins' postseason quest.

Next up in the AFC Championship game were the Pittsburgh Steelers, a team known for their "Steel Curtain" defense. The Steelers presented a formidable challenge, but the Dolphins' versatile attack was ready. Miami's defense, too, rose to the occasion, showcasing the depth of talent and strategic planning that had made them unbeaten. The Dolphins triumphed with a 21-17 victory, a testament to their complete team effort. Key plays, including a pivotal interception by safety Jake Scott, turned the tide in Miami's favor, demonstrating the "No-Name Defense's" critical role in the Dolphins' success.

With the AFC Championship secured, the Dolphins had one final hurdle to clear: Super Bowl VII against the Washington Redskins. The Super Bowl presented the ultimate test of the Dolphins' pursuit of perfection. The Redskins, led by coach George Allen, were a veteran team with a formidable defense and a balanced offense. The stage was set for a historic showdown in Los Angeles on January 14, 1973.

The Dolphins entered the game with a singular focus: to complete their perfect season. The game was a defensive battle, with both teams struggling to find the end zone. Miami's defense, true to form, held the Redskins to minimal gains, showcasing the discipline and teamwork that had defined their season. Offensively, the Dolphins managed to find cracks in the Redskins' defense, with Jim Kiick scoring the only touchdown for Miami. The game's most memorable moment came from a miscued field goal attempt by the Dolphins, which led to the Redskins' only score, ensuring a nail-biting finish.

Despite the Redskins' late score, the Dolphins' defense stood tall in the final moments, securing a 14-7 victory and completing the only perfect season in NFL history. Miami's accomplishment was a testament to their resilience, team spirit, and unmatched skill. The victory in Super Bowl VII was not just a win but a historic moment that etched the 1972 Dolphins into sports history.

The Dolphins' journey to a perfect season was marked by standout performances, strategic mastery, and moments of high drama. Players like Bob Griese, who returned in the Super Bowl to lead his team, and Mercury Morris, whose speed was a weapon throughout the season, were integral to Miami's success. The "No-Name Defense" proved that recognition doesn't come from flashy nicknames but from performance on the field, where it matters most.

The aftermath of the 1972 Miami Dolphins' perfect season was a whirlwind of celebration, reflection, and recognition. Completing an unbeaten season, capped with a Super Bowl victory, etched the team's name in history, setting a standard that has remained unmatched. The achievement transcended the realm of football, becoming a symbol of excellence and determination in the face of challenges.

The Dolphins' perfect season became a source of pride not only for the team and its fans but also for the city of Miami and the broader NFL community. The players, many of whom had been overlooked or underestimated in their careers, found themselves in the spotlight, their contributions finally recognized on a national scale. Coach Don Shula, already respected for his coaching acumen, was celebrated as one of the greatest coaches in the history of the sport, a mastermind who had led his team to the pinnacle of success.

In the years following their perfect season, the Dolphins remained a formidable force in the NFL, returning to the Super Bowl the following year and maintaining a competitive edge throughout the decade. However, the legacy of the 1972 team was about more than just wins and losses. It was about the power of teamwork, the pursuit of excellence, and the belief that perfection was attainable.

The players who made up the 1972 Dolphins went on to have varied careers. Some, like Larry Csonka and Bob Griese, were inducted into the Pro Football Hall of Fame, their contributions to the game forever immortalized. Others, like Mercury Morris and Nick Buoniconti, became advocates for player health and safety, using their platforms to address issues within the sport. The bond forged during that perfect season remained strong, with team members often reuniting to celebrate the anniversary of their historic achievement.

As the years have passed, the 1972 Miami Dolphins have continued to hold a unique place in NFL lore. Each year, as the last unbeaten team in the league suffers its first loss, the surviving members of the '72 Dolphins celebrate, a tradition that has become a light-hearted reminder of their unmatched feat. This celebration is not about gloating but about honoring a moment in time when everything aligned for one team to achieve the impossible.

The impact of the Dolphins' perfect season extends beyond the players and the NFL. It has become a point of reference for excellence and perseverance in sports and other fields. Coaches and players in various sports often cite the Dolphins' season as an example of what can be achieved with hard work, dedication, and a unified team effort.

The echoes of the 1972 Miami Dolphins' perfect season still resonate through the halls of NFL history, a beacon of excellence and a testament to the power of teamwork, discipline, and determination. The achievement of finishing a season undefeated, culminating in a Super Bowl victory, remains unmatched, setting the '72 Dolphins apart as one of the greatest teams in the history of professional football.

The legacy of this perfect season extends beyond the records and the accolades. It became a source of pride for the players who were part of that historic team. Players like Bob Griese, Larry Csonka, and Mercury Morris went down in history not just as exceptional talents but as members of an elite group that achieved what many thought impossible. Coach Don Shula's leadership and vision were instrumental in guiding the Dolphins to perfection, cementing his status as one of the greatest coaches in NFL history.

The '72 Dolphins also left a lasting mark on the culture of football and sportsmanship. They showed that with a clear goal, unwavering commitment, and mutual support, extraordinary results are achievable. Their perfect season became a benchmark of excellence, a lofty goal that teams in every subsequent NFL season have aspired to but have yet to reach.

Beyond the realm of sports, the story of the 1972 Dolphins serves as an inspiration. It's a narrative that resonates with anyone striving to overcome challenges, pursue perfection, and achieve greatness in their endeavors. The Dolphins' journey from the first game of the season to their Super Bowl victory is a powerful reminder of what's possible when talent is combined with hard work, strategic planning, and a never-give-up attitude.

Each year, as the NFL season unfolds and teams vie for the coveted Super Bowl championship, the memory of the Dolphins' perfect season is revisited. When the last unbeaten team finally loses, members of the '72 Dolphins are known to celebrate, not out of spite, but as a commemoration of their unique bond and extraordinary achievement. It's a tradition that underscores the difficulty of their accomplishment and the pride they take in

43

maintaining their unique place in NFL history.

CHAPTER 7:
J.J. Watt: More Than a Player

Talent and hard work can take you far in football, but character, kindness, and community spirit make you a legend. J.J. Watt, one of the most dominant defensive players in NFL history, is a shining example of an athlete who's achieved greatness not just by how he plays on the field but also by how he lives off it.

Justin James Watt, better known as J.J. Watt, began his journey in Waukesha, Wisconsin. From a young age, J.J. showed a passion for sports, but it was football where he truly shined. His journey wasn't a straight path to success; it was filled with hard work, determination, and a relentless drive to improve. Watt played college football at the University of Wisconsin, where his outstanding performances caught the eye of scouts from the National Football League.

In the 2011 NFL Draft, the Houston Texans selected Watt with the 11th overall pick, a decision that would significantly impact the franchise and the city of Houston. Watt's rookie season was impressive, showcasing his abilities and setting the stage for what would become one of the most illustrious careers for a defensive player.

Watt's on-field achievements are nothing short of remarkable. Over his career, he's been named the NFL Defensive Player of the Year three times, a feat matched by only a few players in league history. His combination of size, speed, and intelligence allowed him to disrupt offenses and become a nightmare for quarterbacks. Watt's ability to sack the quarterback, tackle runners in the backfield, and even swat passes out of the air earned him a reputation as a defensive powerhouse.

J.J. Watt's NFL career is studded with standout moments that showcase his dominance on the football field. One of his most memorable seasons came in 2014, a year that solidified his reputation as one of the league's most formidable defensive forces. That season, Watt became the first player in NFL history to record two 20-sack seasons, a staggering achievement that speaks to his ability to disrupt opposing offenses consistently.

Watt's stats from that season alone are enough to dazzle any football fan: 20.5 sacks, 78 total tackles, 4 forced fumbles, and an incredible 5 total touchdowns, including 3 on offense. Yes, you read that right—Watt was so versatile that he occasionally played on offense, catching touchdown passes like a seasoned tight end. This blend of athleticism, skill, and football IQ is rare, making Watt a unique and game-changing player.

But Watt's influence isn't just measured in sacks and touchdowns. In one game against the Buffalo Bills in 2014, Watt showcased his game-changing ability by intercepting a pass and returning it 80 yards for a touchdown. Plays like this not only shifted the momentum of the game but also lifted the spirits of his teammates and fans, showcasing Watt's ability to lead by example.

Despite facing significant injuries throughout his career, including a broken leg and multiple back surgeries, Watt's dedication to the game never wavered. Each time he was sidelined, he focused on his recovery with the same intensity he brought to the field, always aiming to return stronger. His resilience and commitment to rehabilitation serve as a testament to his character, both as a player and a person.

J.J. Watt's career was adorned with individual accolades that underscore his dominance on the football field. Beyond being a three-time NFL Defensive Player of the Year (2012, 2014, 2015), Watt's statistical achievements place him among the all-time greats in defensive play. For instance, in the 2012 season, Watt led the league with a staggering 20.5 sacks, showcasing his ability to disrupt the opposing team's offense single-handedly. But Watt's impact wasn't limited to just sacks; he also recorded 81 tackles, 16 passes defensed, and four forced fumbles that season, displaying his versatility and all-around contributions to the Texans' defense.

Watt's 2014 season was perhaps even more impressive, as he again reached 20.5 sacks, solidifying his reputation as one of the most fearsome pass rushers in the league. That year, Watt became the first player in NFL history to record two 20-sack seasons. His performance was so outstanding that he received votes for the NFL Most Valuable Player award, a rare feat for a defensive player. Watt's ability to change the course of a game made him a focal point of opposing teams' game plans, yet he continued to excel despite the added attention.

Off the field, Watt's story of community service was equally inspiring. His response to Hurricane Harvey in 2017 exemplifies his commitment to helping others. Initially setting a modest fundraising goal of $200,000, Watt's campaign quickly gained momentum, capturing the hearts of people around the world. His transparent and frequent updates on social media about the fundraising efforts and plans for utilizing the funds encouraged even more people to contribute, eventually raising over $41 million. This effort led to the repair and rebuilding of over 1,183 homes, the recovery and distribution of over 239 million meals, and provided healthcare services to many affected by the hurricane.

Watt's philanthropic work extends beyond disaster relief. Through his foundation, he has been deeply involved in supporting youth athletics across the United States. Understanding the role sports played in his own development, Watt's foundation focuses on funding after-school athletic programs for children in underfunded schools and communities. By providing these opportunities, Watt believes in giving children a foundation for success through teamwork, hard work, and perseverance.

The impact of Watt's charitable work can be seen in the smiles of children playing on new sports equipment, in the gratitude of families returning to their rebuilt homes, and in the community spirit that his actions have helped strengthen. Watt's belief in using his platform for good has inspired countless others to give back, creating a ripple effect of kindness and generosity.

J.J. Watt's influence also reached into the locker room and onto the practice field, where his work ethic and leadership inspired teammates and young players alike. Stories of Watt's dedication to his craft, including his intense training regimen and study of game film, have become legendary. His commitment to excellence in all aspects of his life serves as a model for aspiring athletes everywhere.

As the sun set on J.J. Watt's illustrious NFL career in 2022, the sports world paused to reflect on the legacy of a player who redefined the role of a defensive athlete in football. Watt's retirement announcement was met with an outpouring of respect and admiration from fans, teammates, and rivals alike, a testament to the impact he had both on and off the field.

Throughout his career, Watt faced adversity head-on, turning setbacks into comebacks with a resilience that became as much a part of his legacy as his achievements on the field. Despite dealing with significant injuries that would have sidelined lesser athletes, Watt's spirit never wavered. His return to play after each injury illustrated not just physical strength but a mental fortitude that inspired those around him. This perseverance in the face of adversity is a cornerstone of Watt's legacy, teaching us that obstacles are just opportunities for growth.

J.J. Watt's departure from the NFL was a moment of reflection for many. It wasn't just the end of a career for one of the most dominant defensive players in the history of the sport; it was the closing of a chapter for an individual who had profoundly affected the league, his community, and fans worldwide. Watt's journey underscores that greatness is achieved not solely by what is accomplished on the field but by the character shown in the face of challenges and the commitment to making a difference in the lives of others.

In reflecting on J.J. Watt's career, we don't just celebrate the records or the awards; we celebrate a man who embodied the spirit of perseverance, leadership, and altruism. Watt's story is a powerful reminder that being more than a player means leaving an indelible mark on the hearts and minds of people everywhere, showing that with talent, hard work, and a heart for others, it's possible to inspire change far beyond the game. As Watt moves forward into retirement, his legacy continues, encouraging us all to strive for excellence in every arena of life.

CHAPTER 8:
Deion Sanders: Prime Time's Dual-Sport Dynamism

Few names in the history of football shine as brightly as Deion Sanders. Known as "Prime Time" for his ability to deliver spectacular performances when the stakes were highest, Sanders wasn't just a football player; he was a two-sport superstar, excelling in both the National Football League and Major League Baseball. His dynamic presence and unparalleled athleticism made him a legend on the field and an inspiration off it.

Born on August 9, 1967, in Fort Myers, Florida, Deion Sanders grew up with a deep love for sports. It was clear from an early age that Sanders was gifted with extraordinary athletic abilities. However, what set Sanders apart was not just his physical talent but his work ethic and determination to be the best.

Sanders attended Florida State University (FSU), where he didn't just play one sport; he starred in three: football, baseball, and track. His time at FSU showcased his incredible versatility and set the stage for his future professional career. In football, Sanders was a lockdown cornerback, known for his speed, agility, and unparalleled ability to read the game. His skills on the football field were matched by his prowess on the baseball diamond, where he excelled as an outfielder with a powerful arm and lightning-fast base running.

Sanders's college career was filled with highlights and awards, but one of his most memorable moments came in 1988. In a game against Auburn, Sanders returned a punt 89 yards for a touchdown, showcasing his electrifying speed and agility. This play was a glimpse of what was to come in his professional career, where he would become one of the most exciting and dynamic players to watch.

In 1989, Deion Sanders was drafted by both the NFL and MLB, a rare feat that underscored his extraordinary talent in both sports. The Atlanta Falcons selected him in the first round of the NFL Draft, while the New York Yankees picked him in the MLB Draft. Sanders made history by becoming the only athlete to play in both a Super Bowl and a World Series, demonstrating his unique dual-sport capabilities.

Sanders's impact on the football field was immediate. In his rookie season with the Falcons, he returned a punt 68 yards for a touchdown in his very first game. His speed, confidence, and playmaking ability quickly made him one of the most feared defensive players in the league. But Sanders's talents weren't confined to defense alone; he was also a threat on special teams and occasionally played on offense, showcasing his versatility and the broad range of his skills.

Deion Sanders's career in the NFL is a storied tale of game-changing plays and unparalleled athleticism. However, his journey across two major sports leagues showcases his unique place in sports history. After being drafted by the Atlanta Falcons in 1989, Sanders quickly became known for his confidence, flair, and, most importantly, his unmatched skill on the football field. Yet, what truly set Sanders apart was his decision to not only pursue an NFL career but to also play professional baseball with the New York Yankees.

Sanders's NFL career was marked by highlight-reel interceptions, jaw-dropping punt returns, and the occasional offensive play that left fans and opponents in awe. His ability to read quarterbacks and anticipate plays made him one of the most effective cornerbacks in the league. Sanders didn't just defend; he transformed defense into offense, often returning interceptions for touchdowns, a feat that earned him the nickname "Neon Deion."

Throughout his football career, Sanders played for several teams, including the Atlanta Falcons, San Francisco 49ers, Dallas Cowboys, Washington Redskins, and the Baltimore Ravens. His time with the 49ers in 1994 was particularly memorable. That season, Sanders recorded six interceptions, returning them for a total of 303 yards and three touchdowns, earning him the NFL Defensive Player of the Year award. His contributions were pivotal in leading the 49ers to a victory in Super Bowl XXIX, solidifying his reputation as a difference-maker in crucial moments.

Parallel to his NFL career, Sanders also made his mark in Major League Baseball. Playing for teams like the New York Yankees, Atlanta Braves, Cincinnati Reds, and San Francisco Giants, Sanders demonstrated that his athletic prowess was not confined to the gridiron. His speed, which made him a terror for NFL offenses, also made him a formidable base-stealer and an excellent outfielder in baseball. In 1992, while with the Atlanta

Braves, Sanders became the only athlete to play in both a Super Bowl and a World Series, highlighting his incredible dual-sport ability.

Perhaps one of Sanders's most memorable baseball moments came during the 1992 World Series with the Braves. In Game 3, Sanders went 2-for-4 with a walk, showcasing his batting skills and base-running speed. Despite the Braves not winning the championship, Sanders's performance in the World Series was a testament to his remarkable talent and versatility as an athlete.

Sanders's commitment to both sports was not without its challenges. Balancing schedules, training, and the physical toll of competing at the highest levels in two professional sports is a feat few athletes have attempted and even fewer have succeeded at. Sanders's ability to excel in both the NFL and MLB is a testament to his extraordinary talent, work ethic, and determination.

Deion Sanders's influence stretched beyond the impressive statistics and the championships; he redefined what it meant to be an entertainer in sports. Sanders knew that sports were not just about competition; they were also about putting on a show for the fans. With his high-stepping interceptions returns and electrifying punt returns, Prime Time made sure the spotlight was always on him, and he thrived in it. This flair for the dramatic, combined with his undeniable talent, made Sanders a must-watch athlete, whether he was on the diamond or the gridiron.

In football, Sanders's impact was felt every time he stepped onto the field. He had a knack for making big plays in big moments, which is why he was such a valuable asset to his teams.

His tenure with the Dallas Cowboys in the mid-1990s was especially notable. Joining the team in 1995, Sanders helped the Cowboys secure their third Super Bowl victory in four years at Super Bowl XXX. His presence alone shifted the balance of power, as opposing quarterbacks often hesitated to throw the ball his way, effectively taking away half of the field from the offense.

Sanders's ability to shut down top receivers was unmatched, earning him eight Pro Bowl selections and six First-team All-Pro honors throughout his career. But perhaps more impressive was his knack for scoring. Sanders holds the NFL record for career non-offensive touchdowns, finding the end zone on interception returns, punt returns, kickoff returns, and even receiving touchdowns, showcasing his versatility and scoring ability.

On the baseball field, Sanders's speed was his greatest asset. He was a threat to steal bases every time he got on base, keeping pitchers and catchers on edge. His best season came in 1992 when he hit .304, stole 26 bases, and scored 54 runs in just 97 games for the Atlanta Braves. Sanders's baseball career was marked by flashes of brilliance that showed what he could have achieved had he dedicated himself solely to baseball.

Balancing two professional sports careers was a Herculean task that required not just physical strength and talent but also immense mental fortitude. Sanders faced skepticism and criticism from those who thought he should focus on just one sport. However, Prime Time was not one to back down from a challenge. He used the doubts as motivation, pushing himself harder to succeed in both arenas.

Sanders's dual-sport career did not come without sacrifices. The physical toll of playing football and baseball, often in the same year, was immense. Yet, Sanders managed to maintain a high level of play in both sports, a testament to his physical conditioning and dedication to his craft.

As Deion Sanders's playing days in both the NFL and MLB drew to a close, his impact on both sports remained undiminished. His retirement from the NFL came after an illustrious career filled with memorable moments, groundbreaking achievements, and a legacy of being perhaps the most dynamic two-sport athlete the world has ever seen. Sanders officially retired from the NFL in 2005, leaving behind a legacy marked by his unique flair, unmatched athleticism, and a career filled with highlights that will be remembered by fans for generations.

In reflecting on Sanders's career, it's clear that his influence went beyond just the records and the highlight reels. "Prime Time" changed the way athletes are perceived, blending sports performance with entertainment and personality in a way that few had done before. His confidence, often seen as brashness, was actually a deep belief in his abilities and a desire to perform at his best when the lights were brightest.

After his retirement, Sanders didn't step away from the spotlight. Instead, he transitioned to a career in media and ultimately to coaching college football, most recently with the University of Colorado. Sanders has used his platform to mentor young athletes, sharing his experiences and lessons learned from a dual-sport career. His commitment to giving back is evident in his various philanthropic efforts, including work with children and schools to promote education and well-being.

Sanders's induction into the Pro Football Hall of Fame in 2011 was a fitting capstone to his football career, an acknowledgment of his exceptional contributions to the game. His speech, filled with gratitude, humor, and reflections on his journey, highlighted the people and experiences that shaped him. It also reinforced his belief in striving for greatness, regardless of the challenges.

Deion Sanders's legacy is multifaceted. As a player, he was electrifying, a game-changer in the truest sense, whose talents dazzled fans and frustrated opponents. As a person, he's complex—confident yet caring, with a deep sense of responsibility to use his fame for the benefit of others. His dual-sport success stands as a testament to his incredible athletic ability and work ethic, setting a high bar for future generations.

The story of "Prime Time" Deion Sanders is more than just a sports narrative; it's a lesson in determination, the pursuit of excellence, and the power of believing in oneself. Sanders showed that with talent, hard work, and an unwavering confidence, it's possible to achieve greatness on multiple stages. His journey inspires young athletes to dream big, work hard, and never limit their potential to just one field of play.

CHAPTER 9:
The 1985 Chicago Bears: A Defense Like No Other

In the heart of Chicago, during the 1985 NFL season, a team emerged that would forever change the way defense is played in football. The Chicago Bears, led by their innovative coach, Mike Ditka, and defensive coordinator, Buddy Ryan, crafted a team so dominant, especially on defense, that they left an indelible mark on the history of the sport.

The Bears' defense in 1985 was not just good; it was legendary. They were a unit that combined strength, speed, and a deep understanding of the game, turning defensive plays into an art form. This group of players, known for their fierce playing style, was characterized by their ability to intimidate and overpower their opponents.

One of the most iconic aspects of the 1985 Bears was their implementation of the "46 defense," a strategic formation devised by Buddy Ryan. This aggressive defensive scheme overwhelmed offenses with sheer force and strategic placement of players, making it nearly impossible for the opposing team's quarterback to find open receivers or for their running back to find a path through the line. The "46 defense" was named after safety Doug Plank, who wore number 46, and who embodied the tough, relentless spirit of the Bears' defense.

At the heart of this formidable defense were several standout players, each bringing their own unique talents to the team. Mike Singletary, the middle linebacker, was known for his intensity and unmatched football IQ. His leadership on and off the field played a crucial role in the Bears' defensive success. Richard Dent, a defensive end, was a force to be reckoned with, using his speed and power to get past offensive linemen and pressure the quarterback. His efforts during the season earned him the Super Bowl XX MVP.

Another key figure in the Bears' defense was Dan Hampton, who played both defensive end and tackle. His versatility and strength were vital in executing the "46 defense" effectively. The secondary wasn't to be overlooked either, with players like Gary Fencik and Dave Duerson providing solid coverage and support against the pass and the run.

The 1985 Bears' defense was known for its ability to not just stop their opponents, but to score points themselves. They had an uncanny knack for turning interceptions and fumbles into touchdowns, adding an extra layer of threat to their already formidable presence on the field.

This defense was a major factor in the Bears' success throughout the season. They allowed the fewest points in the league, shut out their opponents in an unprecedented two playoff games, and set a then-record for the most sacks in a single season. Their performance was not just effective; it was demoralizing for their opponents, who often found themselves outmatched and outplayed from the first whistle.

The 1985 season saw the Bears' defense dominate the league like no other before. They allowed the fewest points (198), the fewest total yards (4,135), and recorded an impressive 64 sacks. Their ferocity and skill were unmatched, leading them to shut out their opponents in an astounding 11 games throughout the season, including the playoffs.

One of the most memorable games that showcased the Bears' defensive prowess was against the Dallas Cowboys in Week 11. The Bears decimated the Cowboys 44-0, one of the most lopsided victories in NFL history, highlighting their defense's ability to dismantle even the strongest of offenses.

As the regular season gave way to the playoffs, the Bears continued their march with determination. Their defense, relentless and unwavering, was the nightmare of every team that faced them. Fans and opponents alike watched in awe as the Bears carved their path through the postseason, fueled by their revolutionary defense and a collective desire to achieve greatness.

The Chicago Bears' march through the 1985 season had the feeling of destiny about it. Each game seemed not just a step towards the Super Bowl but also a demonstration of how football could be transformed by a defense that was as strategic as it was powerful. The playoffs would provide the perfect stage for the Bears to showcase the full might of their defensive prowess.

Their first playoff game was a divisional matchup against the New York Giants. The Giants, no slouches themselves, were overwhelmed by the Bears' defense. The Bears won convincingly, 21-0, with the defense not allowing a single point. This game was a masterclass in defensive play, with the Bears sacking the Giants' quarterbacks six times and limiting them to a mere 32 rushing yards. The "Monsters of the Midway" were not just stopping their opponents; they were demoralizing them.

But the true test of the Bears' historic defense came in the NFC Championship game against the Los Angeles Rams. Played under the gray, cold January sky of Chicago, the game was less a contest than a coronation. The Bears' defense, led by the ferocious play of Richard Dent, who recorded 1.5 sacks, and Wilber Marshall, who returned a fumble 52 yards for a touchdown, was suffocating. The Rams, like the Giants before them, failed to score a single point. The final score, 24-0, sent the Bears to Super Bowl XX, marking the second game in a row where the defense had pitched a shutout.

The stage was set for the grand finale of the 1985 season: Super Bowl XX, held in New Orleans, Louisiana. The Bears faced the New England Patriots, a team that had fought its way through the playoffs with a strong running game and a capable defense. However, they had not encountered a force like the Bears' defense.

From the outset, the Bears' defense imposed their will on the Patriots. The Patriots' first play from scrimmage set the tone for the day—a sack by Steve McMichael for a loss of seven yards. The Patriots' offense was stifled throughout the game, managing only 123 total yards, the lowest total by any team in Super Bowl history at the time. The Bears' defense forced six turnovers, including two interceptions and four fumble recoveries, showcasing their ability to not just stop their opponents, but to take the ball away and create scoring opportunities.

One of the most iconic moments came when defensive lineman William "The Refrigerator" Perry, known more for his size and blocking than his ball-carrying, scored a touchdown on offense, illustrating the depth of talent and the spirit of fun that characterized the Bears' approach to the game.

The final score of Super Bowl XX was 46-10, a resounding victory for the Bears. Their defense had dominated the postseason, allowing only 10 points over three games, an achievement that remains one of the most impressive in NFL history.

The legacy of the 1985 Chicago Bears extends far beyond their dominating performance in Super Bowl XX. This team, particularly its defense, reshaped the National Football League's landscape and left an indelible mark on the sport's history. Their innovative tactics, sheer physicality, and unbreakable team spirit have become the gold standard for what a defense can achieve.

In the years that followed, members of the 1985 Bears team became ambassadors of the sport, sharing their experiences and lessons learned from that unforgettable season. Mike Singletary, the fierce middle linebacker, transitioned into coaching, imparting the wisdom and intensity he displayed on the field to a new generation of players. Richard Dent, whose performance in 1985 earned him Super Bowl XX MVP honors, continued to be involved in football and community service, demonstrating the impact a player can have beyond their playing days.

The 1985 season also left a cultural impact that transcended the sport. The Bears were not just a team; they were a phenomenon. They captured the imagination of the nation with their charismatic personalities and larger-than-life characters. None was more emblematic of this than William "The Refrigerator" Perry, whose touchdown in Super Bowl XX became one of the game's most enduring moments. The Bears even entered the pop culture lexicon with the "Super Bowl Shuffle," a rap video featuring players from the team. It was a testament to their confidence and a symbol of their place in the broader American culture of the 1980s.

But perhaps the most significant legacy of the 1985 Chicago Bears is the standard they set for excellence. They showed that a great defense could not only win games but could dominate and demoralize opponents. They were a team that played with joy, ferocity, and an unbreakable bond of brotherhood. Future NFL teams striving for greatness looked to the '85 Bears as a model of what could be achieved when talent meets tenacity.

It's important to reflect on how this team's legacy has continued to resonate through the years, not just in the realm of professional football but in the hearts of sports enthusiasts everywhere. The '85 Bears were more than just a team with a stellar defense; they were a cultural phenomenon that captured the essence of an era, embodying the spirit and passion of competition at its finest.

The players of the 1985 Chicago Bears, from the unstoppable Walter Payton to the indomitable Mike Singletary, from the versatile William "The Refrigerator" Perry to the master strategist Buddy Ryan, each contributed to a legacy that has outlasted their time on the field. Their influence can be seen in the way defenses are built and how football is played today. The 46 defense, aggressive and unyielding, remains a topic of study for coaches striving to replicate even a fraction of its effectiveness.

Beyond strategy and gameplay, the 1985 Chicago Bears left a lasting impact on the NFL's cultural landscape. Their unity, charisma, and larger-than-life personalities showed that football was more than a game; it was a shared experience that could unite people, inspire children, and bring joy to millions. The "Super Bowl Shuffle" remains a symbol of their confidence and camaraderie, a reminder that success is best when it can be shared.

The legacy of the 1985 Bears is also a testament to the enduring nature of excellence. Their record-setting season, culminating in a Super Bowl victory, set a benchmark for success that future teams would aspire to reach. It showed that with the right combination of talent, strategy, and heart, extraordinary achievements are possible.

Today, the 1985 Chicago Bears are remembered not just for what they accomplished on the field but for how they made people feel. They were a source of pride for the city of Chicago, a beacon of excellence in the NFL, and an enduring example of how teamwork, dedication, and passion can lead to legendary accomplishments. Their story is one of inspiration, teaching us that greatness is achieved not through individual achievement alone but through collective effort, shared goals, and an unwavering commitment to excellence.

CHAPTER 10:
Breaking Barriers: The Story of Doug Williams

Few stories in football history are as inspiring as that of Doug Williams, the quarterback who broke through barriers and defied expectations to become a legend of the game. Born on August 9, 1955, in Zachary, Louisiana, Williams's journey to NFL stardom was fueled by his love for football, his incredible talent, and his unwavering determination to succeed, despite the obstacles in his path.

From an early age, Williams showed a natural aptitude for football. His arm strength, accuracy, and football IQ set him apart from his peers, making it clear that he had the potential to go far. However, Williams's journey was not without challenges. Growing up in the segregated South, he faced racial barriers that made his path to success more difficult than it was for others. Yet, Williams never let these obstacles deter him; instead, they only strengthened his resolve.

Williams attended Grambling State University, a historically black college in Louisiana, where he played under the legendary coach Eddie Robinson. At Grambling, Williams's talent truly shone. He passed for more than 8,000 yards and 93 touchdowns during his college career, breaking numerous records and gaining national attention. His success at Grambling paved the way for his entry into the NFL, though the road ahead was still fraught with challenges.

In 1978, Doug Williams was drafted by the Tampa Bay Buccaneers, making him the first African American quarterback to be taken in the first round of the NFL Draft. This achievement was a significant milestone, not just for Williams, but for the league as a whole. It marked a step forward in the ongoing struggle for racial equality in professional sports.

Williams's early years with the Buccaneers were marked by highs and lows. He led the team to three playoff appearances and one NFC Championship game, demonstrating his skill and leadership on the field. However, despite his success, Williams was consistently one of the lowest-paid starting quarterbacks in the league. Contract disputes eventually led to his departure from the Buccaneers in 1983.

Williams's career then took him to the United States Football League (USFL) before he returned to the NFL with the Washington Redskins in 1986. It was with the Redskins that Williams would etch his name into NFL history, overcoming adversity to achieve greatness on football's biggest stage.

The 1987 NFL season was a pivotal chapter in Doug Williams's career and a defining moment in the history of professional football. Joining the Washington Redskins after his stint in the USFL, Williams was initially a backup quarterback. However, his talent, experience, and leadership qualities were undeniable, and he soon found himself in a position to change the course of NFL history.

The Redskins' journey through the 1987 season was marked by ups and downs, but the team, under head coach Joe Gibbs, showed resilience and determination. Williams's role on the team became increasingly important, and his leadership both on and off the field was instrumental in guiding the Redskins through the challenges of the season.

Williams's moment to shine came in the postseason. After leading the Redskins to victories in the divisional playoffs and the NFC Championship game, Williams and his team earned a spot in Super Bowl XXII against the Denver Broncos. This game would not only be the culmination of the season's efforts but also a historic moment for Williams and the NFL.

As the first African American quarterback to start in a Super Bowl, Williams was aware of the significance of the moment. The pressure was immense, not just to perform well but to represent the hopes and aspirations of countless individuals who saw in him a symbol of progress and possibility. The start of the game was challenging for Williams and the Redskins, as they quickly found themselves trailing the Broncos.

However, what happened next is etched in NFL history as one of the most remarkable comebacks in Super Bowl history. After a slow start and despite suffering a knee injury early in the game, Williams unleashed a performance for the ages. In the second quarter alone, he threw four touchdown passes, a Super Bowl record. His arm strength, accuracy, and poise under pressure were on full display as he led the Redskins to score 35 points in a single quarter, another Super Bowl record.

Williams's performance in Super Bowl XXII was not just a showcase of his skill as a quarterback; it was a statement. He finished the game with 340 passing yards and four touchdowns, earning the Super Bowl MVP award. This achievement was a testament to his perseverance, talent, and determination to overcome obstacles.

The impact of Williams's performance in Super Bowl XXII went far beyond the final score. He had shattered a significant barrier, proving that an African American quarterback could lead his team to the ultimate victory in the NFL. His success challenged stereotypes and opened doors for future generations of quarterbacks.

The aftermath of Super Bowl XXII reverberated far beyond the confines of the football field, casting Doug Williams not just as a champion in the realm of sports but as a pivotal figure in the ongoing narrative of racial progress in America. His groundbreaking performance and Super Bowl MVP award were more than personal triumphs; they served as beacons of hope and symbols of change for many.

In the wake of the Super Bowl, Williams was celebrated not only for his exceptional skill as a quarterback but also for his role in breaking down racial barriers within the sport. His success challenged long-standing prejudices and stereotypes about the capabilities of African American quarterbacks at the highest levels of competition. Williams's achievement opened the door wider for future generations of players, making it a little easier for those who would follow in his footsteps.

Despite the magnitude of his success, Williams remained humble and focused on the broader impact of his achievements. He understood that his story was part of a larger struggle for equality and representation in all areas of life, not just sports. Williams used his platform to speak out on issues of racial inequality and to advocate for greater opportunities for young athletes of all backgrounds.

After his historic Super Bowl win, Williams continued his career in the NFL, both on and off the field. Though he would never again reach the heights of that incredible 1987 season, his influence within the sport remained profound. After retiring as a player, Williams transitioned into coaching and executive roles, where he continued to impact the game and mentor young players.

Williams's legacy is evident in the increasing diversity among NFL quarterbacks in the years since his Super Bowl victory. Today, many of the league's top quarterbacks are African American, a testament to the slowly changing attitudes and increasing opportunities within the sport. Players like Patrick Mahomes, Lamar Jackson, and Kyler Murray have followed in Williams's footsteps, leading their teams with skill, intelligence, and poise.

Beyond the gridiron, Williams's story has inspired countless individuals to pursue their dreams, regardless of the obstacles they may face. His journey from a small town in Louisiana to Super Bowl MVP is a testament to the power of perseverance, resilience, and the courage to challenge the status quo.

Doug Williams's remarkable journey and his historic Super Bowl XXII victory not only changed the course of his life but also left an indelible mark on the sport of football and American society. Williams's success in the NFL served as a powerful counter-narrative to the prevailing stereotypes that had long limited opportunities for African American quarterbacks. By shattering these barriers, Williams opened doors and broadened horizons for the next generation of athletes.

In the years that followed his triumph, Williams dedicated himself to mentoring young players and using his experience to foster diversity and inclusion within the sport. His transition into coaching and executive roles in football allowed him to directly influence the development of players, ensuring that the lessons he learned on and off the field would be passed on to future generations.

Williams's impact is also reflected in his work outside the realm of football. He has been involved in various charitable efforts and community service projects, aiming to uplift those in underserved communities. Through educational programs and sports clinics, Williams has sought to inspire young people to achieve greatness, regardless of the challenges they may face.

His legacy is one that transcends his achievements on the football field. It's about the courage to pursue one's dreams, the resilience to overcome adversity, and the strength to challenge and change deeply entrenched stereotypes. Williams's story is a testament to the power of determination and the profound impact that one individual can have on breaking down barriers and opening doors for others.

Doug Williams's story is not just about football; it's a narrative of progress, a chapter in the ongoing story of the struggle for equality and representation. Williams demonstrated that with talent, determination, and the courage to challenge the status quo, it's possible to change perceptions and create new opportunities for those who come after.

CHAPTER 11:
The Evolution of Tom Brady: From Late-Round Draft Pick to GOAT

In the grand history of NFL quarterbacks, one story stands out, a tale of determination, resilience, and unmatched success. This is the story of Tom Brady, a player whose journey from an overlooked draft pick to the Greatest of All Time (GOAT) encapsulates the essence of pursuing dreams with unwavering commitment.

Born on August 3, 1977, in San Mateo, California, Tom Brady's passion for football was evident from a young age. As a kid, he attended San Francisco 49ers games, idolizing legendary quarterback Joe Montana. Brady's dream was not just to play in the NFL but to excel and leave an indelible mark on the sport.

Despite his love for the game and his high school successes, Brady's path to NFL stardom was not straightforward. He faced challenges right from the start, beginning with his college career at the University of Michigan. At Michigan, Brady was not the starting quarterback initially. He had to compete fiercely for playing time, showing early on his resilience and refusal to give up. His college career was a mix of highs and lows, but through hard work and perseverance, Brady emerged as a leader on the team, setting the stage for what was to come in his professional career.

The 2000 NFL Draft was a turning point in Brady's life, though not in the way most future stars experience. Despite his collegiate successes, Brady was not highly sought after by NFL teams. He was selected by the New England Patriots as the 199th overall pick in the sixth round, a moment that many would see as a setback. However, Brady saw it as an opportunity—a chance to prove himself and to show the world that he belonged at the highest level of football.

Brady's early years with the Patriots were about patience and learning. As a backup quarterback, he watched and learned from his teammates, absorbing the intricacies of the NFL game and preparing for when his opportunity would come. And come it did, in the 2001 season, when starting quarterback Drew Bledsoe was injured. Brady stepped in, and the rest, as they say, is history.

In that 2001 season, Brady led the Patriots to their first Super Bowl victory, showcasing his leadership, poise, and ability to perform under pressure. This was just the beginning of what would become one of the most storied careers in NFL history.

Tom Brady's initial Super Bowl win in the 2001 season was far from a fairy-tale ending; it was the beginning of a legendary career that would redefine excellence in the NFL. Brady's journey is a testament to his relentless pursuit of improvement, a quality that has kept him at the top of the game for over two decades.

Following his breakthrough season, Brady didn't rest on his

laurels. Instead, he pushed himself harder, driven by a desire to prove that his success wasn't just a stroke of luck. His work ethic, attention to detail, and mental toughness became hallmarks of his approach to football. Brady's preparation for games was meticulous, studying hours of game footage to understand opponents' tendencies and find ways to outsmart them.

Brady's leadership on and off the field played a pivotal role in the New England Patriots' dynasty. Under his guidance, the Patriots won six Super Bowl titles (XXXVI, XXXVIII, XXXIX, XLIX, LI, and LIII), a record for any quarterback in NFL history. Each victory was a chapter in Brady's ever-growing legacy, showcasing his ability to lead his team to victory in the most critical moments.

One of Brady's most memorable Super Bowl comebacks came in Super Bowl LI against the Atlanta Falcons. The Patriots trailed 28-3 in the third quarter, facing what seemed an insurmountable deficit. Yet, Brady's calm demeanor and unwavering belief in his team's ability to win ignited one of the most incredible comebacks in Super Bowl history. The Patriots won 34-28 in overtime, and Brady's performance—completing 43 of 62 passes for 466 yards—earned him his fourth Super Bowl MVP award.

Brady's achievements are not limited to Super Bowl victories. He has amassed numerous NFL records, including most career wins by a quarterback, most career touchdown passes, and most career passing yards. His longevity and consistency at the highest level of play are unparalleled, with multiple MVP awards and Pro Bowl selections highlighting his individual excellence.

Beyond the statistics and the records, Brady's influence

extends to his teammates and coaches. His leadership style, characterized by encouragement, accountability, and a team-first attitude, has fostered a winning culture wherever he's played. Brady's ability to inspire those around him to reach their highest potential is perhaps as significant a part of his legacy as his on-field achievements.

After stepping into the spotlight in 2001 and guiding the New England Patriots to a Super Bowl victory, Tom Brady's career trajectory shifted dramatically. The world began to witness the rise of a quarterback who would redefine excellence at the position. Yet, it was Brady's relentless pursuit of improvement and his unmatched competitive spirit that propelled him to heights previously unseen in the NFL.

In the seasons that followed his first Super Bowl win, Brady solidified his status as the cornerstone of the Patriots' dynasty. With Coach Bill Belichick at the helm, Brady and the Patriots crafted a legacy of success that dominated the NFL. Brady's leadership on and off the field became legendary. His ability to rally his team in crucial moments led to countless come-from-behind victories, earning him a reputation as a clutch performer.

By the mid-2000s, Brady had already secured three Super Bowl titles, setting numerous records along the way. Yet, his hunger for success never waned. Each season, Brady returned with the same determination and work ethic that defined his early years, constantly seeking ways to elevate his game. His preparation, attention to detail, and understanding of the game were unparalleled, making him a master at reading defenses and making the right calls under pressure.

Brady's approach to the game also evolved over the years. He became an advocate for physical and mental wellness, adopting a strict diet, exercise, and recovery regimen that allowed him to perform at an elite level well into his 40s. This commitment to maintaining his physical condition and his sharp mental focus became a hallmark of Brady's career, setting a new standard for longevity in the sport.

One of Brady's most remarkable seasons came in 2007 when he led the Patriots to an undefeated regular season, a feat achieved by only one other team in the Super Bowl era. That year, Brady threw for a then-record 50 touchdown passes, showcasing his incredible talent and the potent offense he commanded. Although the Patriots fell short in the Super Bowl, Brady's performance throughout the season was a testament to his excellence.

As the years passed, Brady continued to amass accolades and championships. His partnership with Coach Belichick and the Patriots became one of the most successful in sports history, culminating in six Super Bowl titles together. Brady's ability to adapt, his unyielding will to win, and his leadership qualities were the driving forces behind the Patriots' sustained success.

In 2020, the NFL and its fans witnessed a monumental shift that few could have predicted: Tom Brady, the cornerstone of the New England Patriots' dynasty, chose to leave the team with which he had achieved unprecedented success. His decision to join the Tampa Bay Buccaneers marked the beginning of a new chapter, not just for Brady but for the entire league. This move raised questions and sparked debates among fans and analysts alike. Could Brady replicate his success away from New England and Coach Belichick? Would the GOAT continue to shine in a new environment?

Brady's first season with the Buccaneers answered those

questions with a resounding yes. At the age of 43, when most players have long since retired, Brady demonstrated that his competitive fire burned as brightly as ever. Joining a talented but underachieving Buccaneers team, he quickly became the leader they needed, both on the field and in the locker room. His work ethic, experience, and sheer determination lifted the entire organization, transforming the Buccaneers into a championship contender.

The 2020 season saw Brady adapt to a new system under Head Coach Bruce Arians and build chemistry with a new group of talented receivers, including Mike Evans and Chris Godwin, as well as reuniting with his longtime Patriots teammate Rob Gronkowski. Despite the challenges posed by a new team and the global pandemic, which limited offseason workouts and preseason preparation, Brady's performance was stellar. He threw for 4,633 yards and 40 touchdowns, leading the Buccaneers to an 11-5 record and securing a playoff berth.

Brady's leadership and performance shone brightest in the postseason. The Buccaneers won three road playoff games, including a victory over the Green Bay Packers in the NFC Championship game, earning a spot in Super Bowl LV. The stage was set for one of the most remarkable achievements of Brady's career.

In Super Bowl LV, held at the Buccaneers' home stadium in Tampa, Florida—the first time in NFL history a team played the Super Bowl in their home stadium—Brady and the Buccaneers faced off against the defending champions, the Kansas City Chiefs, led by the dynamic young quarterback Patrick Mahomes. The game was billed as a clash of generations, pitting the established GOAT against a rising star who many see as his potential successor.

The Buccaneers, led by Brady's efficient and effective performance, dominated the Chiefs, winning 31-9. Brady threw for 201 yards and three touchdowns, earning his fifth Super Bowl MVP award and, more importantly, his seventh Super Bowl ring, more than any player in NFL history. This victory was a testament to Brady's unparalleled career, showcasing his ability to lead, adapt, and succeed, no matter the circumstances.

The story of Tom Brady, which spans over two decades in the National Football League, is a narrative of unyielding perseverance, unparalleled success, and the relentless pursuit of greatness. As we conclude this chapter, we reflect on the legacy of a player who, through sheer determination and an unwavering belief in himself, rose from the 199th draft pick to stand atop the NFL as the GOAT.

After his monumental victory in Super Bowl LV with the Tampa Bay Buccaneers, Brady continued to defy the limitations of age, returning for another season that further solidified his status as an enduring icon of the sport. Each game he played was a testament to his exceptional skill, leadership, and the timeless appeal of his competitive spirit. Yet, even legends have their final chapters, and for Tom Brady, that moment came in 2023 when he announced his retirement from professional football.

Brady's decision to retire marked the end of an era not just for the Buccaneers but for the entire NFL. His impact on the game, characterized by his record seven Super Bowl victories, five Super Bowl MVP awards, and numerous passing records, is unparalleled. Beyond the accolades and the statistics, however, lies Brady's true legacy—the inspiration he provided to athletes around the world. His story is a powerful reminder that greatness is not preordained but earned through hard work, resilience, and an unwavering commitment to excellence.

Throughout his career, Brady was more than just a quarterback; he was a mentor, a leader, and a champion for the sport. He changed the way the game is played and perceived, elevating those around him and setting a new standard for what it means to be a professional athlete. His meticulous preparation, dedication to physical and mental wellness, and strategic approach to the game have influenced countless players across the league, shaping the next generation of NFL stars.

As we reflect on Tom Brady's illustrious career, it's clear that his influence extends far beyond the football field. He has become a cultural icon, embodying the spirit of determination and the joy of competition. Brady's retirement in 2023 was not just the conclusion of an individual's career but a moment for the sports world to pause and celebrate one of its greatest champions.

Tom Brady's journey from a draft pick to the GOAT is a story of triumph, a narrative that will continue to inspire long after his playing days are over. It's a reminder that with passion, perseverance, and a relentless pursuit of one's goals, any dream is within reach. As future generations of athletes lace up their cleats and step onto the field, they carry with them the legacy of Tom Brady—a legacy of greatness, hard work, and the enduring belief that anything is possible.

CHAPTER 12:
The Greatest Show on Turf: The 1999 St. Louis Rams

At the end of the twentieth century, in the bustling city of St. Louis, Missouri, a football team took the field and changed the game forever. This team wasn't just any team; it was the 1999 St. Louis Rams, a group of players who would come together to create one of the most unforgettable seasons in NFL history. Their story is not just about winning games; it's about how they played the game with such flair, speed, and precision that they earned the nickname "The Greatest Show on Turf."

The 1999 season started with uncertainty. The Rams hadn't had a winning season in over a decade, and their hopes seemed to hang by a thread when Trent Green, their starting quarterback, suffered a season-ending injury during a preseason game. But as fate would have it, this setback paved the way for an unknown backup quarterback named Kurt Warner to step onto the field. Warner, who had once stocked shelves in a grocery store and played in the Arena Football League, was about to embark on a journey from obscurity to stardom.

Under the guidance of head coach Dick Vermeil and

offensive coordinator Mike Martz, the Rams' offense transformed into a high-flying, unstoppable force. Warner's arm, combined with the talents of running back Marshall Faulk, wide receivers Isaac Bruce and Torry Holt, and an innovative playbook, made the Rams' offense the most exciting in the league. They played on artificial turf, which suited their game perfectly, allowing their speed and agility to shine even brighter.

Throughout the regular season, the Rams lit up scoreboards like a pinball machine. Kurt Warner threw for a staggering 4,353 yards and 41 touchdowns, earning him the NFL MVP award. Marshall Faulk, a versatile and dynamic running back, contributed over 2,000 combined rushing and receiving yards, creating nightmares for opposing defenses. Together, with the explosive receiving duo of Bruce and Holt, the Rams offense became a spectacle, drawing fans from all over to witness their breathtaking performances.

Game after game, the Rams demonstrated their dominance, finishing the regular season with a record of 13-3. Their offense wasn't just good; it was historic, setting records and redefining what was possible in the NFL. They scored 526 points that season, an average of over 32 points per game, showcasing their ability to outscore any opponent.

The Rams' journey through the regular season was a rollercoaster of emotions, filled with thrilling victories and nail-biting finishes. Each player on the team contributed to their success, embodying the spirit of teamwork and determination. The defense, though often overshadowed by the offense, played with grit and toughness, making key stops and turnovers that kept the Rams in games.

As the regular season gave way to the playoffs, the Rams

were poised to make a run at the Super Bowl. But the road to the championship would test their resolve, their skills, and their belief in each other.

As the playoffs dawned, the 1999 St. Louis Rams, fueled by their historic regular-season performance, were ready to prove that they were not just a sensational offense but a team capable of clinching the ultimate prize—the Super Bowl. The city of St. Louis buzzed with excitement, and fans across the country tuned in to see if the Rams could continue their high-scoring ways against the pressure of playoff football.

The Rams' first playoff game was a Divisional Round matchup that would test their mettle. Their opponent, the Minnesota Vikings, were no strangers to high stakes, boasting a powerful offense of their own. However, the Rams, playing in front of their home crowd, were undeterred. The game quickly turned into a showcase of the Rams' explosive potential. Kurt Warner's precise passing, Marshall Faulk's dynamic playmaking, and the receiving corps' speed and agility were on full display, propelling the Rams to a convincing victory. The defense, often seen as the team's Achilles' heel, stepped up significantly, making crucial stops and showcasing a toughness that many had overlooked.

Buoyed by their success in the Divisional Round, the Rams advanced to the NFC Championship game, where they faced a formidable Tampa Bay Buccaneers team known for its stingy defense. This game was a classic showdown between an unstoppable force and an immovable object. Early on, it became clear that points would be at a premium, a departure from the high-scoring affairs the Rams were accustomed to. The Buccaneers' defense managed to slow down the Rams' aerial attack, turning the game into a defensive struggle.

However, the hallmark of a great team is the ability to find a way to win, even when their strengths are neutralized. Late in the game, with the outcome hanging in the balance, Warner connected with receiver Ricky Proehl for a touchdown, the game's only visit to the end zone. The Rams' defense held firm in the final moments, securing a hard-fought 11-6 victory and a ticket to Super Bowl XXXIV.

The stage was set for a dramatic conclusion to the Rams' magical season. Their opponent in the Super Bowl was the Tennessee Titans, a team that had also enjoyed a remarkable season and was making its first Super Bowl appearance. The matchup promised to be an epic battle, with the Rams' high-powered offense facing off against the Titans' balanced attack and sturdy defense.

As Super Bowl XXXIV kicked off, the anticipation reached a fever pitch. Fans of the sport and casual observers alike were captivated by the storyline of the Rams' Cinderella season. Could the team that had risen from obscurity to dominate the NFL complete their fairy tale run with a Super Bowl victory?

Super Bowl XXXIV was more than just a championship game for the Rams; it was the culmination of a season that had captured the imagination of football fans everywhere. The Georgia Dome in Atlanta was buzzing with excitement as the Rams prepared to face the Tennessee Titans, a team as determined and resilient as they were.

The game lived up to its billing, with both teams showcasing why they had made it to the NFL's grandest stage. For the Rams, the first half was a demonstration of their powerful offense, with

Kurt Warner connecting on deep throws and Marshall Faulk making significant plays. However, the Titans were no pushovers, countering with their own scoring drives. The game was a tightly contested affair, with neither team able to gain a decisive advantage early on.

As the game progressed, the Rams' "Greatest Show on Turf" began to shine. Warner found wide receiver Isaac Bruce for a 73-yard touchdown, a play that highlighted the Rams' ability to strike quickly and decisively. Yet, true to the spirit of a championship game, the Titans rallied back, displaying their own brand of toughness and tenacity.

The drama reached its peak in the game's final moments. The Titans, trailing by a touchdown, were driving down the field, inching closer to a potentially game-tying score. With just seconds remaining and the Titans on the Rams' 10-yard line, the entire season came down to one final play. Titans quarterback Steve McNair snapped the ball and completed a pass to wide receiver Kevin Dyson, who darted towards the end zone.

What happened next would become one of the most memorable plays in Super Bowl history. Rams linebacker Mike Jones made a game-saving tackle on Dyson just one yard short of the end zone as time expired. This incredible defensive play sealed the victory for the Rams, 23-16, and crowned them Super Bowl champions. The image of Dyson stretching towards the goal line only to be stopped short captured the essence of the game—a battle of inches, fought with every ounce of strength and determination.

Kurt Warner was named Super Bowl MVP, capping off an incredible season with a 414-yard passing performance, the second-highest in Super Bowl history. His journey from grocery store clerk to Super Bowl champion was now complete, a testament to perseverance and belief in oneself.

The Rams' victory in Super Bowl XXXIV was more than just a win; it was the pinnacle of a season that defied expectations and delighted fans with its style, grace, and sheer excitement. "The Greatest Show on Turf" had proven that they were indeed the best team in the NFL, combining a high-octane offense with timely plays on defense to achieve football immortality.

The legacy of the 1999 St. Louis Rams, known affectionately as "The Greatest Show on Turf," transcends their Super Bowl XXXIV victory. This team captivated the hearts of fans not just with their success, but with the way they played the game. They brought an offensive dynamism and flair to the NFL that was, at the time, revolutionary. Their story is one of transformation, teamwork, and the realization of seemingly impossible dreams.

In the aftermath of their Super Bowl win, the Rams continued to be a force in the NFL for several seasons, thanks to the foundation laid during that magical 1999 campaign. The offensive strategies employed by Coach Dick Vermeil and offensive coordinator Mike Martz changed how teams approached the game, placing a greater emphasis on passing and scoring. Kurt Warner, Marshall Faulk, Isaac Bruce, and Torry Holt became household names, inspiring a generation of players to emulate their style and success.

The legacy of the Rams' 1999 season also lies in the hope it gave to underdog teams and players. Kurt Warner's journey from undrafted free agent to NFL MVP and Super Bowl champion is a testament to perseverance and belief in one's abilities. It's a story that resonates with anyone who has ever faced long odds and dared to dream big.

Furthermore, the Rams' success helped to transform the city of St. Louis, uniting the community and bringing joy to countless fans. The team's impact was felt not just in the stands of the Edward Jones Dome but throughout the city, as they became a symbol of excellence and the power of collective effort.

Today, the legacy of the 1999 St. Louis Rams lives on in the NFL's continued evolution into a more offense-driven league. Their record-setting performance during that season set new standards for what an offense could achieve and paved the way for the high-scoring, pass-oriented game we see today.

CHAPTER 13:
USC vs. Texas: A Battle of Titans at the Rose Bowl

In the world of college football, some games are so epic, they're talked about for years, becoming part of the sport's rich history. One such game is the 2006 Rose Bowl, where the University of Southern California (USC) Trojans faced off against the University of Texas Longhorns. This wasn't just any game—it was a clash of titans, a battle for the ages, featuring two unbeaten teams vying for the national championship.

The stage was set in Pasadena, California, at the historic Rose Bowl stadium. The USC Trojans, led by coach Pete Carroll, were the defending national champions and boasted two Heisman Trophy winners in their ranks: quarterback Matt Leinart, who won the Heisman in 2004, and running back Reggie Bush, the 2005 recipient. USC was on a 34-game winning streak, aiming to secure their place as one of the greatest teams in college football history.

On the other side, the Texas Longhorns, under the guidance of coach Mack Brown, had their sights set on their first national championship since 1970. Leading the charge for Texas was quarterback Vince Young, a phenomenal athlete whose dynamic playmaking ability had dazzled fans all season. The Longhorns were undefeated too, and they arrived in Pasadena determined to dethrone the reigning champs.

As kickoff approached, excitement reached fever pitch. Fans from all over the country tuned in to watch these two college football powerhouses go head to head. The game lived up to its billing right from the start, with both teams showcasing why they were undefeated. USC's powerful offense, led by Leinart and Bush, faced off against Texas's equally formidable attack, orchestrated by the unstoppable Vince Young.

The first half was a back-and-forth battle, with both teams scoring touchdowns and demonstrating their offensive prowess. But it was Vince Young's electrifying performance that kept fans on the edge of their seats. Whether he was throwing pinpoint passes or weaving through the USC defense with his runs, Young was the centerpiece of Texas's strategy.

As the game progressed, the tension mounted. Each drive, each play, felt like it could tip the balance of this titanic clash. The Trojans and Longhorns traded blows, with the lead changing hands multiple times. The skill, determination, and heart of both teams were on full display, making this game a classic from the moment it began.

As the second half of the 2006 Rose Bowl game unfolded, the USC Trojans and Texas Longhorns continued their fierce battle, with each team showcasing their stars and the depth of their talent. The game had already seen its fair share of spectacular plays, but it was clear that both teams had more to give.

For USC, quarterback Matt Leinart, who had thrown for over 3,000 yards and 28 touchdowns that season, was a steadying presence. His connection with wide receiver Dwayne Jarrett, who had racked up 1,274 receiving yards and 16 touchdowns, was particularly dangerous. Meanwhile, Reggie Bush, known for his electrifying speed and agility, added another dimension to USC's offense. Bush had amassed over 1,700 rushing yards and scored 16 touchdowns that season, making him a focal point of Texas's defensive game plan.

On the Texas side, Vince Young was the linchpin of the Longhorns' offense. Young's ability to both pass and run had been a nightmare for defenses all season. By the end of the year, Young had thrown for 3,036 yards and 26 touchdowns, while also rushing for 1,050 yards and 12 touchdowns. His performance in the Rose Bowl was shaping up to be one for the ages, as he consistently found ways to move the ball against the Trojans' defense.

One of the game's pivotal moments came in the fourth quarter. USC, leading by 12 points with just minutes remaining, seemed poised to secure their third consecutive national championship. However, Vince Young and the Longhorns refused to go quietly. Young led Texas on a crucial drive, culminating in a touchdown that brought the Longhorns within five points of USC.

With time winding down, Texas needed a defensive stop to have any chance of completing the comeback. The Longhorns' defense rose to the occasion, forcing USC into a critical fourth-down situation. In a bold move, Pete Carroll opted to go for it on fourth and two, but the Texas defense held strong, stopping USC short of the first down and giving the ball back to Young and the offense with a chance to win the game.

What followed would become one of the most iconic sequences in college football history. Vince Young, with calm and determination, guided Texas down the field. Facing a fourth and five with just 19 seconds left on the clock, Young took the snap, scrambled to his right, and dashed into the end zone for a touchdown, giving Texas a 41-38 lead.

As the final seconds ticked away, the magnitude of what had just happened began to sink in. Texas had completed an incredible comeback, led by Vince Young's heroic performance. Young finished the game with 267 passing yards, 200 rushing yards, and three rushing touchdowns, including the game-winner, solidifying his legacy as one of the greatest to ever play in a college football championship.

The 2006 Rose Bowl was more than just a game; it was a display of heart, skill, and the indomitable will to win. Players like Matt Leinart, Reggie Bush, Vince Young, and Dwayne Jarrett had all left their mark on this epic showdown, contributing to a contest that fans would never forget.

The aftermath of the 2006 Rose Bowl was a whirlwind of celebration, reflection, and recognition of the incredible feats achieved on the field. Texas's victory not only secured them the national championship but also ended USC's hopes of a three-peat, a testament to the intense competition and high stakes that define college football.

The impact of the game extended beyond the immediate joy of victory and the sting of defeat. It resonated throughout the college football world, highlighting the excellence of two top programs and the incredible talent of the players involved. Vince

Young's performance, in particular, was lauded as one of the greatest in college football history. His ability to lead his team to victory against a formidable opponent solidified his place in the pantheon of college football legends.

For Texas, the win represented the culmination of years of hard work, dedication, and belief in the team's ability to achieve greatness. Head Coach Mack Brown received widespread praise for his leadership, having guided the Longhorns to their first national championship in over three decades. The victory in Pasadena was more than just a win; it was a moment that united the Texas community and fans around the world in celebration of a remarkable achievement.

On the other side, the USC Trojans faced the difficult task of reconciling with a heart-wrenching loss. Despite the outcome, the team's accomplishments over the season and in previous years remained a source of pride. Players like Matt Leinart, Reggie Bush, LenDale White, and Dwayne Jarrett had etched their names into USC lore, contributing to a legacy of excellence that would inspire future generations of Trojans.

The 2006 Rose Bowl also left a lasting legacy on the sport itself, setting a benchmark for what a championship game could be. It was a reminder of the unpredictable nature of football, where determination and resilience could turn the tide in the most dramatic fashion. The game became a case study in the importance of never giving up, no matter the odds, a lesson that resonated with players, coaches, and fans alike.

This monumental clash not only showcased the pinnacle of athletic excellence but also imparted lessons in perseverance, teamwork, and the indomitable human spirit that resonate with fans to this day.

Vince Young's legendary performance, where he amassed 267 passing yards and an astonishing 200 rushing yards, underscored his pivotal role in Texas's victory. His final touchdown, a breathtaking 8-yard run on fourth and five, is a play replayed in the minds of football fans everywhere, a testament to individual brilliance and the sheer will to win.

For USC, the combined efforts of stars like Matt Leinart, who threw for 365 yards, and Reggie Bush, with 82 rushing yards and a crucial 26-yard touchdown reception, highlighted the Trojans' formidable challenge to the Longhorns. Despite their loss, USC's contributions to this classic encounter helped elevate the game to legendary status, demonstrating the depth of talent and strategic gameplay that college football embodies.

The 2006 Rose Bowl wasn't just a game; it was a showcase of record-breaking performances and a thrilling narrative of competition at its finest. It set a standard for what championship football could be, with both teams combining for over 1,100 total yards in a back-and-forth contest that kept fans on the edge of their seats until the very end.

In reflecting on the 2006 Rose Bowl, we celebrate not only the incredible achievements of the players and the unforgettable moments of the game but also the spirit of college football that brings people together in shared excitement and admiration. The USC vs. Texas showdown at the Rose Bowl remains a beacon of the heights that sports can reach, inspiring future generations to dream big, work hard, and cherish the journey as much as the destination.

CHAPTER 14:
Josh Allen: Rising Above the Doubts

In the wide-open spaces of Firebaugh, California, a young boy named Josh Allen had a dream that seemed as big as the sky above his family's farm: to play quarterback in the NFL. But Josh's journey was filled with challenges right from the start. Despite his undeniable talent and love for football, he didn't turn many heads in high school. His town was small, his school was smaller, and opportunities to shine were limited.

Josh's high school days ended with little fanfare in the world of college football recruiting. With no scholarship offers from major universities, his path to football stardom seemed more like a fading dream than an achievable goal. Yet, Josh didn't give up. He took his talents to Reedley College, a junior college where he hoped to prove himself. And prove himself he did. With a powerful arm and a determination as strong as steel, Josh began to turn heads.

In just one season at Reedley, Josh's performances on the field were a testament to his hard work and raw talent. He threw passes with precision, scrambled with unexpected agility, and led his team with a quiet confidence that belied his years. It was here that Josh started to believe more deeply in himself, even if the big-name colleges still hadn't taken notice.

Finally, the University of Wyoming did. They saw potential in Josh, a diamond in the rough that they were willing to polish. Moving to Wyoming was a big step for Josh, far from his California home, but it was a step he took without hesitation. The Cowboys' football program offered him the chance to play Division I football, and Josh grabbed it with both hands, determined to make the most of this opportunity.

At Wyoming, Josh faced new challenges. The weather was colder, the competition tougher, and the stakes higher. But with each game, Josh grew stronger, more confident, and more skilled. He dazzled fans with his arm strength, throwing the football farther than anyone thought possible, and impressed coaches with his understanding of the game.

However, Josh's college career wasn't without its ups and downs. He faced injuries and tough losses, moments that tested his resolve and made him question his path. Yet, it was these challenges that forged his character, teaching him the resilience and perseverance he'd need to reach the NFL.

Josh's journey at Wyoming wasn't just about the touchdowns he threw or the games he won; it was about overcoming doubt—doubt from others and doubt in himself. With each throw, each run, and each game, Josh was not just playing football; he was building a foundation for his future, a future he once could only dream of.

Josh Allen's time at the University of Wyoming set the stage for the next big leap in his journey: the NFL Draft. As his college career neared its end, Josh's dream of playing in the NFL seemed closer than ever. Yet, as the draft approached, so did the doubts. Critics questioned his accuracy, his decision-making, and whether his success in college could translate to the professional level. The doubts were loud, but Josh's determination was louder.

In the months leading up to the draft, Josh dedicated himself to improving every aspect of his game. He worked tirelessly with coaches and trainers, refining his technique, studying the intricacies of NFL offenses, and preparing himself mentally and physically for the challenges ahead. Josh knew that to succeed at the next level, he needed to be his best self, and nothing was going to stop him from getting there.

On draft day in 2018, tension and excitement filled the air. Josh, surrounded by his family, waited for the call that would change his life. Then, it came. The Buffalo Bills selected Josh Allen as the seventh overall pick, placing their trust and their future in his hands. It was a moment of validation, a dream realized, but Josh knew it was just the beginning of an even bigger challenge.

Arriving in Buffalo, Josh was met with a new set of challenges. The NFL was faster, more complex, and more competitive than anything he'd faced before. In his rookie season, Josh showed flashes of brilliance, using his strong arm to make impressive throws and his athleticism to evade defenders and gain yards on the ground. However, he also faced struggles, as every rookie does, learning from each game and using those lessons to grow.

Josh's commitment to improvement was evident. With each passing season, he has evolved as a quarterback. His accuracy improved, his decision-making became sharper, and his leadership on and off the field has grown stronger. Josh's hard work has paid off, and the Bills have become a force to be reckoned with in the NFL, much of it thanks to their young quarterback's dedication and skill.

By his third season, Josh had led the Bills to the playoffs and was establishing himself as one of the exciting young talents in the league. His ability to make big plays, whether with a deep pass or a scramble for a crucial first down, energized the team and the fans. Doubts about his potential were being replaced by admiration for his performance and anticipation for what he could achieve next.

With each season, Josh Allen has continued to silence his critics and exceed expectations. His arm strength was undeniable, but it was his improvement in accuracy and decision-making that truly marked his development as one of the NFL's elite quarterbacks. Allen's ability to learn from mistakes, embrace coaching, and tirelessly work on his craft during the offseason began to pay dividends on the field.

One of the most significant aspects of Allen's game is his dual-threat capability. Not only can he launch the ball deep with precision, but he can also use his athleticism to evade defenders, extending plays and rushing for critical yards. This versatility makes him a unique challenge for opposing defenses and adds a dynamic layer to the Buffalo Bills' offense.

Off the field, Allen's impact is equally profound. His commitment to the Buffalo community, his involvement in charitable activities, and his approachable, humble demeanor endeared him to fans and citizens alike. Josh Allen is not just a quarterback for the Buffalo Bills; he is a beacon of hope and a source of pride for the city of Buffalo.

Josh Allen's journey embodies the spirit of perseverance. From being a doubted high school player to facing skepticism as a draft pick, Allen's path to NFL stardom was fraught with challenges. Yet, his story is a testament to what can be achieved with hard work, resilience, and an unyielding belief in oneself.

Josh Allen's legacy is still being written, with each game adding to his story of overcoming doubts to achieve greatness. His journey reminds us that success is not handed out but earned, and that the greatest victories often come after the hardest battles. For young fans and aspiring athletes, Josh Allen's rise from obscurity to the upper echelons of the NFL serves as inspiration to chase their dreams, no matter the odds.

Allen's tale is more than just a football story; it's a narrative of rising above doubts, pushing through adversity, and emerging stronger on the other side. As Josh Allen continues to build his legacy, his impact extends beyond the gridiron, inspiring a new generation to believe in the power of perseverance and the possibility of achieving their own version of greatness.

CHAPTER 15:

Super Bowl LI: The Greatest Comeback

In the world of sports, some moments are written into history not just for the outcome, but for the journey to that outcome. Super Bowl LI, played on February 5, 2017, is one such moment. It wasn't just a game; it was a dramatic tale of perseverance, teamwork, and an incredible comeback that left fans around the world in awe.

The game pitted the Atlanta Falcons against the New England Patriots, two teams that had fought hard to earn their place in the NFL's biggest showdown. The Falcons, led by their MVP quarterback Matt Ryan, boasted one of the league's most explosive offenses. The Patriots, guided by the legendary quarterback Tom Brady, were no strangers to the Super Bowl stage, having won four titles prior to this game.

As the game kicked off in Houston's NRG Stadium, anticipation was high. The first half was dominated by the Falcons, who quickly showcased their offensive firepower. They soared to a 21-3 lead by halftime, leaving fans and commentators wondering if the game was already decided. The Falcons' defense was equally impressive, stifling the Patriots' attempts to build momentum and seemingly securing their path to a Super Bowl victory.

But if there's one thing sports history teaches us, it's that no lead is safe until the final whistle. The Patriots, known for their resilience, started the second half facing a daunting challenge. Yet, within their locker room, there was belief. Led by Brady, one of the greatest quarterbacks in NFL history, the Patriots were about to embark on a comeback for the ages.

The third quarter saw the Falcons extend their lead to 28-3, a margin that seemed insurmountable. However, the Patriots remained unfazed. With Brady at the helm, they slowly chipped away at the Falcons' lead. The Patriots' defense tightened, giving Brady and the offense more opportunities to score. Slowly, the momentum began to shift.

As the Patriots scored touchdown after touchdown, the sense of disbelief began to grow among fans and players alike. Each successful drive by the Patriots was a testament to their determination and skill. The Falcons fought valiantly to stem the tide, but the Patriots' surge was relentless.

By the end of the fourth quarter, the Patriots had erased a 25-point deficit, tying the game at 28-28 and sending Super Bowl LI into overtime—a first in Super Bowl history. The comeback was complete, but the game was not yet won. The stage was set for a dramatic conclusion to one of the most memorable games in NFL history.

As Super Bowl LI moved into overtime, the air was thick with tension and anticipation. For the first time in Super Bowl history, the game would be decided in this high-stakes format, where every play could shift the fate of the championship. The New England Patriots, having completed one of the most remarkable comebacks in NFL history, won the coin toss and elected to receive the ball, giving them the first chance to score in overtime.

The atmosphere in NRG Stadium was electric as Tom Brady and the Patriots offense took the field. With the momentum firmly on their side, they began their drive with confidence and precision. Brady, whose experience and calm under pressure had been critical in getting the Patriots to this point, led his team with a series of successful passes. The Falcons' defense, which had been so dominant in the first half, faced the challenge of stopping a rejuvenated Patriots team.

In overtime, every move was critical. The Patriots methodically moved the ball down the field, showcasing their balanced attack. Key receptions by wide receivers Julian Edelman and Danny Amendola, combined with effective runs by running back James White, brought the Patriots closer to the end zone and the championship.

The climax of the game—and the season—came when James White, who had already scored two touchdowns in the game, received a pass from Brady and pushed his way into the end zone for the game-winning touchdown. The stadium erupted as Patriots players, coaches, and fans celebrated the incredible victory. The Falcons, despite their impressive performance for much of the game, were left to reflect on how the championship had slipped through their fingers.

Super Bowl LI's final score, 34-28, marked the largest comeback in Super Bowl history. Tom Brady, who orchestrated the incredible turnaround, was named Super Bowl MVP for a record fourth time. His performance, which included 466 passing yards, solidified his legacy as one of the greatest quarterbacks in NFL history.

The Patriots' victory in Super Bowl LI was more than just a testament to their skill on the field; it was a demonstration of resilience, teamwork, and the never-give-up attitude that defines champions. For the Falcons, the loss was heartbreaking, but it also provided valuable lessons in the importance of perseverance and the relentless pursuit of excellence.

In the days and weeks following Super Bowl LI, the sports world buzzed with discussions about the game's historic nature. The Patriots' astonishing comeback was analyzed and celebrated, not just by fans of the team but by anyone who appreciated the drama and unpredictability of sports. Tom Brady and the Patriots had not only secured another championship but had also delivered a performance that would be remembered for generations.

The impact of Super Bowl LI extended beyond the record books. For the New England Patriots, the victory further solidified their legacy as one of the NFL's greatest dynasties. It was a testament to the leadership of Coach Bill Belichick, the skill and resilience of Tom Brady, and the depth and talent of the team's roster. The Patriots' culture of discipline, preparation, and mental toughness was credited with laying the foundation for their ability to overcome such a significant deficit.

For the Atlanta Falcons, the outcome of Super Bowl LI was a heartbreak that would linger. The team had played brilliantly for much of the game, showcasing their own offensive firepower and defensive prowess. Quarterback Matt Ryan, the season's MVP, and the Falcons had given their all on the NFL's biggest stage, only to fall just short of the championship. The loss served as a painful reminder of the challenges of closing out a game against a formidable opponent. Yet, it also provided valuable lessons and motivation for the team and its fans. The Falcons' performance in Super Bowl LI, despite the outcome, underscored the talent and potential within the team.

The greatest comeback in Super Bowl history also offered lessons about the importance of perseverance, belief, and teamwork. It reminded players, coaches, and fans alike that no game is over until the final whistle and that with determination and unity, remarkable achievements are possible. Young athletes around the world drew inspiration from the Patriots' comeback, seeing in it a metaphor for overcoming challenges in sports and in life.

Super Bowl LI also highlighted the essential role of preparation and adaptability in achieving success. The Patriots' ability to adjust their game plan and execute under pressure was a critical factor in their comeback. This adaptability, coupled with the team's unwavering belief in their ability to win, showcased the strategic elements of football and the mental toughness required to compete at the highest level.

As the story of Super Bowl LI takes its place in NFL history, its impact continues to resonate far beyond the confines of NRG Stadium on that unforgettable February evening. The game stands as a monument to the spirit of competition, a vivid illustration of why millions around the globe cherish sports for the drama, the excitement, and the lessons they impart about human potential.

The Patriots' unprecedented comeback in Super Bowl LI serves as an enduring beacon of hope and resilience, not just for athletes but for anyone facing seemingly insurmountable odds. It reminds us that with determination, teamwork, and belief in oneself, the impossible can become possible. Tom Brady's leadership and the collective effort of the entire Patriots team during those final moments of the game underscore the power of unity and the importance of never giving up, regardless of the circumstances.

For young fans and aspiring players, Super Bowl LI is a masterclass in perseverance. It teaches that success is not always linear and that setbacks can be the prelude to triumph if faced with courage and resolve. The game is a testament to the importance of preparation, adaptability, and mental toughness—qualities that are valuable not only on the football field but in every aspect of life.

The legacy of Super Bowl LI also extends to the Atlanta Falcons, who, despite the heartbreaking loss, showcased incredible talent, teamwork, and sportsmanship. The Falcons' journey to the Super Bowl and their performance for much of the game serve as a reminder of the fine margins between victory and defeat and the importance of playing with heart and passion until the final whistle.

Super Bowl LI will forever be remembered as a testament to the incredible feats that are possible when individuals come together with a shared purpose and refuse to accept defeat. It's a narrative that will continue to inspire, teach, and entertain, reminding everyone that in the game of football, as in life, anything is possible when you believe and persevere.